S0-AUY-108

KEYS TO BUSINESS AND PERSONAL FINANCIAL STATEMENTS

Nicholas G. Apostolou
Professor
Louisiana State University

BARRON'S

New York • London • Toronto • Sydney

Copyright © 1991 by Barron's Educational Series, Inc.

All rights reserved.
No part of this book may be reproduced
in any form, by photostat, microfilm, xerography,
or any other means, or incorporated into any
information retrieval system, electronic or
mechanical, without the written permission
of the copyright owner.

All inquiries should be addressed to:
Barron's Educational Series, Inc.
250 Wireless Boulevard
Hauppauge, New York 11788

Library of Congress Catalog Card No. 90-28588

International Standard Book No. 0-8120-4622-6

Library of Congress Cataloging-in-Publication Data
Apostolou, Nicholas G.
    Keys to business and personal financial statements
/ Nicholas G. Apostolou.
        p.   cm.
    Includes index.
    ISBN 0-8120-4622-6
    I. Financial statements.   I. Title.
HF5681.B2A7   1991
657'.3—dc20   90-28588
                                                        CIP

PRINTED IN THE UNITED STATES OF AMERICA
1234 9770 987654321

CONTENTS

1

INTRODUCTION

Accounting is a system of providing financial information about economic entities for use by business managers and potential investors in making economic decisions. Accounting's primary functions are to record, classify, and summarize financial transactions, culminating in the preparation of financial statements.

Financial statements are the primary means by which businesses communicate their financial position and the results of operations. There are four main financial statements—the balance sheet, the income statement, the retained earnings statement (sometimes expanded into a statement of stockholders' or owners' equity), and the statement of cash flows. These statements provide information about a business's financial health and about significant changes in its resources and obligations in a format useful to decision makers.

While the importance of financial statements to businesses is obvious, such statements can also be very useful to individuals wishing to monitor their own financial well-being. You need financial statements, especially a balance sheet and an income statement, to keep track of your current financial condition and assess your progress in achieving your financial goals. Managing your money without financial statements is like navigating without a compass: you don't know where you are and you can't determine your progress toward your goal. Understanding and using personal financial statements is critical to effective personal financial planning.

This book discusses both business and personal financial statements. Many people are intimidated by financial statements and, as a result, ignore them. Financial statements, which can seem extremely complex, are based upon certain accounting rules with which you should be familiar; once you learn the basic rules and terms, the statements seem much less formidable. The goal of this book is to help you become proficient in understanding and interpreting financial statements.

2

BOOKKEEPING

Financial accounting is the process of identifying, measuring, and communicating financial information about economic events. Bookkeeping is that aspect of the accounting process that focuses on measuring the results of a firm's activities. The bookkeeping process starts with transactions (economic events that are accounted for and reflected in financial statements) and results in financial statements. Whether the bookkeeping system is manual or computerized, it adheres to the same basic principles. The process can be represented as follows:

Transaction→Journal→Ledger→Financial Statements

The process starts with the identification and quantification of a transaction. Transactions are analyzed to determine their effect on the balances of a firm's assets, liabilities, and owners' or stockholders' equity. For example, the purchase of inventory on credit requires the recording of the asset acquired (inventory) and the liability incurred (called accounts payable).

Transactions are initially recorded in a journal, also called the "book of original entry," which is a day-by-day listing of all business transactions engaged in by the firm. Transactions are then recorded in (or "posted to") a ledger, a specialized record used to classify the journal entries based on their characteristics. For example, most ledgers have separate accounts for journal entries involving cash, for entries involving sales, and for entries involving items such as inventory, marketable securities, and bound payable. In most manual bookkeeping systems, each account is a separate page in a book that resembles a loose-leaf binder. Accounts are usually arranged in the following sequence: assets, liabilities, owners' or stockholders' equity, revenues, and expenses.

In its simplest form, a ledger account is shaped like a T and is therefore often called a "T account." It usually takes the following form:

Account Title	
Debit side	Credit side

The left-hand side of a T account is called the debit side, and the right-hand side is called the credit side. The account title is usually indicated atop this T-shaped chart.

Which side of an account is to be used to record increases and which side for decreases depends upon the nature of the account (asset, liability, or owners' equity). The rules for entering debits and credits are as follows:

Assets: Increases in assets are recorded on the debit side, whereas decreases are recorded on the credit side.

Liabilities: Increases in liabilities are recorded on the credit side of an account, whereas decreases are debited.

Owners' Equity: Increases in owners' equity are recorded as credits, decreases as debits.

The reason debits and credits are defined differently for assets, liabilities, and owners' equity is that the system is structured so that total debits must always equal total credits. Assets are recognized differently from liabilities and owners' equity because they are on opposite sides of the accounting equation:

$$Assets = Liabilities + owners' equity$$

4

To illustrate:

Assets			Liabilities			Owners' Equity	
Debit	Credit	=	Debit	Credit	+	Debit	Credit
Increase	Decrease		Decrease	Increase		Decrease	Increase

For example, suppose $100 of inventory was purchased on credit (called accounts payable). Using T accounts, we could analyze the transaction as follows:

Inventory		Accounts Payable	
100			100

The increase in cash is recorded as a debit entry to the cash account, and an increase in accounts payable is recorded as a credit entry to the accounts payable account, with total debits (100) equalling total credits (100). Debits and credits must always be equal; if they are not, a clerical error has occurred. Each entry made in recording a transaction must consist of at least one account that is credited and one that is debited.

At the end of every accounting period, financial statements are prepared. The bookkeeping procedures illustrated above are vital to this process, because the most important accounting statements—the balance sheet and the income statement—are derived from journal and ledger entries.

3

CONCEPTS UNDERLYING BUSINESS FINANCIAL STATEMENTS

In order to understand accounting methods and financial statements completely, you should understand the broad concepts and conventions that underlie financial accounting and reporting. Keep in mind, however, that accounting is not a science. Most of these concepts and conventions are not logically deduced; rather, they are derived from existing practice.

The following description of concepts is not meant to be exhaustive. The concepts included in this discussion were selected because of their critical importance to understanding the basic techniques of accounting.

- **Going concern.** A company is assumed to be in business indefinitely unless there is evidence to the contrary. This assumption underlies the depreciation and amortization of assets over their useful lives. If a company expects to liquidate in the near future, its assets are valued at their worth at liquidation rather than original cost.
- **Historical cost.** Under the historical-cost assumption, accountants have traditionally valued most assets at their original or acquisition cost. This cost is the most objective and reliable measure of an asset's value. Many critics say that assets and liabilities should be

reflected at their current market value in the financial statements. Although accountants do not deny the usefulness of knowing the current value of a firm's assets and liabilities, they balk at the difficulty in implementing this method of valuation. The current market value of an asset may be difficult to determine (a fifty-year-old steel plant, for example) or may be subject to varied opinions (mineral deposits and timberland, for example). Accountants advocate the use of historical cost because it represents an objective and verifiable method of valuation.

Matching. The matching concept states that if specific revenues are recognized in a period, the expenses incurred in generating those revenues should also be assigned to that period. Income is recognized by subtracting from revenues the expenses incurred in generating those revenues. The matching concept does not imply that revenues always equal expenses; revenues represent the accomplishments of the business, whereas expenses are a measure of the effort required to produce the revenue. Matching is an ideal that cannot always be realized, because there is no direct link between some expenses and revenues. For example, it is sometimes difficult to match the cost of a plant with revenues produced by selling products.

Conservatism. The conservatism principle applies to judgments made in uncertain situations; if alternative values are possible and the accountant is uncertain about which to choose, it supports the choice of the option least likely to overstate assets and profits. The conservatism convention does not mean that assets or income should be deliberately understated; its intent is simply to provide a guide to decisionmaking in uncertain situations.

Time period. To provide timely information about a company's progress, it is useful to prepare periodic performance reports. The most commonly used time periods are the month, the quarter, and the year. Because the production and sale of products is an ongoing process, assigning a company's activities to artificial time periods depends on estimates. The shorter the time period, the less reliable is the measure of performance; thus, a monthly report is usually less reliable than a quarterly, and a quarterly report is usually less reliable than an annual report.

Money measurement. Accounting is based on the assumption that money is an appropriate basis for accounting measurement and analysis. Only transaction data capable of being expressed in monetary terms are included in the accounting records of a business. Thus, the monetary unit is assumed to be the best way to communicate the results of the business's production and exchange activities.

Materiality. An item is material if it can influence or change the judgment of a reasonable person. When the amounts of money involved are material, the transaction must be accounted for according to generally accepted accounting principles (GAAP); when the amounts are immaterial, GAAP becomes less significant. Materiality is a matter of relative size and importance. For example, GAAP states that the cost of long-lived assets should be spread over the useful life of these assets by recognizing a portion of the cost as depreciation expense each year. General Motors, however, expenses the cost of wastebaskets (that is, deducts the full cost when it is incurred), even though they may have long lives. This policy is acceptable because the cost of wastebaskets is immaterial to General Motors.

Consistency. Financial statements are most useful when information about a company is measured and disclosed in the same manner from one accounting period to the next. Similarly, accounting information is most helpful when it can be used to evaluate the progress of a single business over time and when the results of different businesses can be compared with each other. Comparisons are made easier when businesses follow the same set of accounting principles over time. Consistency does not preclude changing from one generally accepted method to another generally accepted method, but if such a change is made, the company must disclose the nature of and reason for the change and its dollar effects.

Full disclosure. Accountants strive to reveal information that is of sufficient importance to influence the judgment and decisions of an informed user. Complying with this convention requires a trade-off between completeness and understandability. Accountants do not want to overwhelm the user with unessential detail. The importance of full disclosure is the reason the footnotes contained in financial statements are considered to be an integral part of the statements.

4

CORPORATIONS

There are three primary forms of business organizations in the U.S. economy: proprietorships, partnerships, and corporations. Of the three, the corporation has become by far the most dominant. In 1990, about 60 percent of the country's gross national product originated in nonfinancial corporations. Nearly all the largest industrial firms are corporations. Corporations have assumed a commanding role in the economy because of their facility for attracting and accumulating large amounts of capital; few individuals possess the resources to build and sustain the large industrial complexes required to carry on business in the current economic environment.

Corporations can be classified according to the following characteristics:

1. Ownership
    - Public corporations—governmental units or business operations owned by governmental units, such as municipal transit systems.
    - Private corporations—corporations that are privately owned.
    - Nonstock—nonprofit organizations that do not issue stock, such as colleges and churches.
    - Stock—companies that issue stock and seek to generate profits.
2. Ownership interests
    - Closed corporations—corporations wherein capital stock is not available for public purchase and is held by a few stockholders.
    - Open corporations—publicly held corporations

with stock available for public purchase on an exchange or over the counter.

The United States has no federal incorporation laws; authority to grant corporate charters is vested in individual states. Most states have adopted the principles recommended in the Model Business Corporation Act of 1959 and, as a result, the laws governing specific requirements for stock issuance, definition of legal capital, limitations on dividends, constraints on treasury stock, and provisions for the retirement of treasury stock (common stock bought back by the corporation) are very similar from state to state.

To establish a corporation, its owners must file articles of incorporation with the proper department of the government of the state in which incorporation is desired. When this process is completed, the corporation charter is issued and the corporation is recognized as a legal entity subject to the laws of the state of incorporation.

The corporate form of ownership has several advantages that have helped make it dominant in the American economy:

1. Limited liability. The limited liability feature, which limits the extent of a stockholder's possible loss to the value of the property or service invested, is crucial to the success of the corporate form of organization. Stockholders, the owners of a corporation, contribute either property or services to the entity in return for ownership shares. If the corporation incurs losses to the extent that its remaining assets are not sufficient to pay its creditors, the personal assets of the individual stockholders cannot be attached by creditors; whereas if a partnership or proprietorship cannot meet its obligations, creditors have recourse against the personal assets of the owners. Limited liability allows corporations to raise funds easily from individuals and institutions.

2. Unlimited life. Corporations are assumed to have an unlimited life span unless specified otherwise. Unlike

11

a proprietorship or partnership, a corporation is not terminated by the death or incapacity of an owner.

3. Transferability of interest. Ownership in corporations is represented by shares of stock that can be freely bought and sold with little or no effect on the operations of the corporation.

4. Corporate management. Corporations can hire well-qualified management personnel even if they are not stockholders.

Corporations do have some disadvantages, including:

1. Double taxation. The profits generated by corporations are subject to federal income taxes. Dividends distributed to stockholders from these profits are taxed as personal income to the stockholder. As a result, the federal government taxes corporate profits twice.

2. Government regulation. Corporations are subject to greater regulation than partnerships or proprietorships.

5

THE BALANCE SHEET: AN OVERVIEW

A company's balance sheet is like a snapshot; it provides a picture of the financial health of a business at a certain point in time. Essentially, a balance sheet reveals what a business has, what it owes, and how much money the owners have invested in the business. The items of value that a firm owns or controls are called *assets*. *Liabilities* represent the claims of creditors against these assets. The value of the assets in excess of the total of the liabilities is called *owners' equity, shareholders' equity,* or *stockholders' equity;* in other words, owners' equity represents the owners' claim to the assets of a business net of its liabilities. The periodic preparation of a balance sheet containing assets, liabilities, and owners' equity helps the owners to identify and analyze trends in the business's finances, for example, by disclosing conditions, such as buildups of inventory or receivables (amounts due from customers), that may require immediate manager attention.

At any given time, the assets of a business equal the total claims against those assets by its creditors and owners. This relationship is contained in the balance sheet or accounting equation, which is expressed as follows:

$$\text{Assets} = \text{Liabilities} + \text{Owners' Equity}$$

where assets are the total amount invested in assets of the business, liabilities are the amount supplied to the business by its creditors, and owners' equity is the amount supplied to the business by its owners.

A simple example will illustrate this formula. Suppose John Jones starts a business. He has $10,000 cash in the bank for use by the business. This amount was obtained by investing $5,000 of his own money and by borrowing $5,000 from a bank. At this point, the balance sheet formula is as follows:

Assets	=	Liabilities	+	Owners' Equity
$10,000	=	$5,000	+	$5,000

All businesses basically use the same categories of assets, liabilities, and owners' equity. Assets are listed on one side of the balance sheet in decreasing order of liquidity, that is, the ease with which they can be converted into cash. Liabilities are listed on the other side in the order in which they must be repaid. Owners' equity is listed after liabilities. (See Exhibit 1 at the end of this Key).

Assets can be classified into three categories: current assets; property, plant, and equipment; and other assets. *Current assets* include cash and other assets expected to be used within one year, such as marketable securities, accounts receivable, notes receivable, inventories, and prepaid expenses. The distinction between current assets and noncurrent assets is important to lenders, because the total of the current assets provides an indication of the amount of cash that could be raised quickly to pay off current liabilities.

Property, plant, and equipment includes business assets that have relatively long lives. These assets are typically not for resale and are used in the production or sale of other goods and services. Examples are land, plant, equipment, machinery, furniture, and fixtures. These assets are disclosed in the balance sheet at their cost less a deduction for the total depreciation recognized on the asset (called accumulated depreciation).

14

EXHIBIT 1

THE CRUMBLEY COMPANY
Balance Sheet
August 31, 1991

ASSETS		LIABILITIES AND OWNERS' EQUITY	
Current Assets:		Current Liabilities:	
Cash	$ 10,000	Accounts Payable	$15,000
Accounts Receivable	50,000	Notes Payable	10,000
Inventory	100,000	Accrued Expenses	5,000
Total Current Assets	160,000	Total Current Liab.	30,000
		Owners' Equity	200,000
Fixed Assets:			
Equipment	90,000		
Less: Accumulated			
Depreciation	(20,000)		
		Total Liabilities	
Total Assets	$230,000	and Owners' Equity	$230,000

Other assets include the company's investments in securities, such as stocks and bonds, and intangible assets (valuable rights) such as patents, franchise costs, and copyrights.

Liabilities, the claims of creditors, are divided into two classes. *Current liabilities* are the amounts owed to creditors that are due within one year, such as accounts payable, notes payable, and accrued liabilities (wages, taxes). *Long-term liabilities,* on the other hand, are claims of creditors that do not come due within one year. Included in this category are mortgages, bonded indebtedness, and long-term bank loans.

Owners' equity, the claims of owners against the business, is a residual amount computed by subtracting liabilities from assets. Its balance is increased by any profits and reduced by any losses incurred by the business.

Assets are discussed in detail in the next Key; liabilities and owners' equity are covered in Key 7.

6

BALANCE SHEET: ASSETS

Accounts are records maintained for each asset, liability, and owners' equity component of an organization. The balance sheet discloses the balances in various asset, liability, and owners' equity accounts at a particular point in time. (However, it does not tell you why the balances in these accounts have changed since the end of the last accounting period. This information can be gotten from the income statement and the cash flow statement.) For larger firms, assets can be divided into five categories: current assets, long-term investments, property, plant, and equipment, intangible assets, and other assets.

Current Assets Current assets (primarily cash, temporary investments, accounts receivable, inventory, and prepaid expenses) are presented on the balance sheet in order of decreasing liquidity, starting with cash.

Cash includes funds that are immediately available for use without any restrictions, such as currency, funds deposited in a bank, checks, money orders, petty cash, and bank drafts.

Temporary investments (sometimes called marketable securities) are those investments that meet two criteria: (1) the investment must be readily marketable (be easily sold at about the current price), and (2) management must intend to sell the investment within one year. The most common form of temporary investment is a government security. (Temporary investments are discussed in detail in Key 14.)

Accounts receivable represents amounts owed to the company by its customers as a result of sales. These receivables, which result from credit granted to customers, may be interest-bearing charge accounts, or they may be interest-free. They are disclosed on the balance sheet at the amount expected to be collected from the customers. (Accounts receivable are covered further in Key 15.)

Inventory is defined as those tangible goods that are held for sale to customers in the ordinary course of business or that are to be consumed in the production of goods and services that are to be sold. Only salable items are included in inventory; they are valued at cost or market value, whichever is lower. (Inventory is discussed more fully in Key 16.)

Prepaid expenses are assets paid for in advance of their use or consumption, such as insurance premiums, rent, and taxes. Prepaid insurance, for example, provides a valuable protection for a company—i.e., is an asset—and the unused portion can be refunded. When the period for which the insurance was purchased has passed, the prepaid insurance premium is deducted from revenue as an expense.

Investments Long-term investments, usually referred to simply as investments, can be broken down into three types:

1. Investments in securities, such as bonds or common stock

2. Investments in tangible, long-term assets not currently used in operation, such as land held for speculation

3. Investments in subsidiaries or affiliated companies

Long-term investments, presented on the balance sheet just below current assets, are usually held for many years (unlike temporary investments, which are by definition sold within one year). Although many long-term investments are readily marketable, management's intention to retain them for more than one year prevents their inclusion among current assets.

Property, Plant, and Equipment Property, plant, and equipment includes durable assets acquired for long-

17

term use in a business, including physical property such as land, buildings, equipment, machinery, furniture, and tools. All of these assets, except land, are subject to depreciation (the decline in utility of an asset as a result of the passage of time or use). For accounting purposes, depreciation is recognized by allocating part of the cost of the asset as depreciation expense each year until the entire cost of the asset is deducted. The total depreciation expense recognized on the asset since acquisition is called accumulated depreciation and is deducted on the balance sheet (see Exhibit 2 at the end of this key). The cost less accumulated depreciation of an asset is referred to as its book value.

This topic is discussed more fully in Key 18.

Intangible Assets   Intangible assets are long-term assets that lack physical substance and are used in the regular operations of a business. Examples of intangible assets include patents, copyrights, trademarks, franchises, goodwill, and royalty arrangements. Part of the cost of these assets is recognized as an expense each year and is deducted on the income statement until the entire cost of the intangible asset is written off. This process, which is similar to the recognition of depreciation, is called amortization.

Intangible assets are the topic of Key 17.

Other Assets   Items included under other assets vary widely in practice. This category usually consists of long-term prepayments that do not fit into any of the other classifications. Examples include long-term advances to company officers, deposits made to secure future contracts, and organization costs.

18

EXHIBIT 2

JONES CORPORATION
Balance Sheet
December 31, 1991

ASSETS

Current Assets:		
Cash		$ 34,000
Temporary investments		10,000
Accounts receivable		15,000
Merchandise inventory		25,000
Prepaid expenses		5,000
Total current assets		89,000
Investments:		
Investments in common stock		25,000
Property, plant and equipment:		
Factory	500,000	
Less: Accumulated Depreciation	(100,000)	400,000
Machinery	100,000	
Less: Accumulated Depreciation	(30,000)	70,000
Intangible assets:		
Patents		4,000
Total Assets		$588,000

7

BALANCE SHEET: LIABILITIES AND OWNERS' EQUITY

The right side of a balance sheet is composed of liabilities and owners' equity. Liabilities and owners' equity represent the claims against the assets of the business; liabilities are the claims of creditors to the assets, and owners' equity is the claims of owners to the assets after the liabilities have been satisfied.

Liabilities   Liabilities, a business's debts, are divided on the balance sheet into current and long-term liabilities. Current liabilities are those claims of outsiders on the business that will fall due within one year. Some of the more important current liability items are the following:

• **Accounts payable**—the amounts owed to suppliers of goods and services from whom the business has bought items on credit. This category includes any items of inventory, supply, or capital equipment purchased on credit and for which payment is expected in less than one year.

• **Notes payable**—loans from individuals, banks, or other lending institutions that fall due within a year. Notes payable differ from accounts payable in that the debt is more formal in nature and is evidenced by a promissory note.

• **Current maturities of long-term debt**—the portion of long-term debt that is payable within one year. Because a liability is classified as current if it is to be paid within a year of the balance-sheet date, any portion of a long-term borrowing that is to be repaid within that time is reclassified from the long-term liability section of the balance sheet to the current liability section.

• **Accrued liabilities**—obligations that the business has incurred but for which no formal bill or invoice has been received. An example of accrued liabilities are accrued taxes, those that are accumulating each day but do not yet have to be paid.

The excess of total current assets over current liabilities—the amount that would remain if all current obligations were paid immediately—is referred to as working capital. Although working capital is seldom disclosed on the balance sheet, it is used by bankers and other creditors as an indication of the short-run liquidity of the company.

Long-term liabilities are debts payable more than one year after the balance sheet date. For many nonfinancial firms, long-term debt accounts for as much as half of their capital structure (the mix of debt and owners' equity used to finance the firm's assets). Included in this category are bonded indebtedness, mortgages, and long-term loans from individuals, banks, and other parties.

Owners' Equity The owners' equity section of the balance sheet is presented below liabilities on the right side of the balance sheet (see Exhibit 3 at the end of this key). Note that the term owners' equity is replaced by shareholders' or stockholders' equity when referring to a corporation. Owners' equity for a small business typically involves a single entry; the shareholders' equity section of a corporation is considerably more complicated.

The shareholders' equity section of the balance sheet is usually divided into three parts:

• **Capital stock**—the par value of the shares issued
• **Additional paid-in capital**—primarily the difference between par value and the amount realized from the sale of the stock
• **Retained earnings**—the undistributed earnings of the corporation

Capital stock is the general term for both common stock and preferred stock. Common stockholders are the ultimate owners of the corporation and have claim to all the assets of the corporation after all liabilities and preferred stock claims have been satisfied. In addition, common stockholders elect the members of the corporation's board of directors.

Preferred stock has several debtlike features and carries a limited claim on assets in the event the company is dissolved. Preferred stock usually does not carry a voting privilege but does receive preference over common stock on dividend distributions (payouts of corporate earnings to shareholders) and on claims on assets in the event the corporation is liquidated.

Par value has no significance with respect to common stock and provides no indication of the market value of the stock. Generally, it is an arbitrarily assigned amount determined when the corporation was originally organized. The amount of par value reported on the balance sheet is the par value of the stock multiplied by the number of shares issued. Any difference between par value and the amount received from the sale of the stock is recorded as additional paid-in capital.

Retained earnings refers to earnings of the corporation that have been retained for use in the business rather than distributed to the shareholders as dividends. Retained earnings should not be confused with cash; they are earnings that have been invested largely in additional assets—such as property, plant, and equipment—in an effort to generate future revenues for the business.

EXHIBIT 3

JONES CORPORATION
Balance Sheet
December 31, 1991

LIABILITIES AND OWNERS' EQUITY

Current Liabilities:	
Accounts payable	$ 55,000
Notes payable	25,000
Accrued liabilities	15,000
Total Current Liabilities	95,000
Long-term Liabilities:	
Mortgage note payable	75,000
Total liabilities	170,000
Stockholders' Equity:	
Preferred stock	50,000
Common stock $2 par value	$285,000
Additional paid-in capital	50,000
Retained earnings	43,000
Total Shareholders' Equity	428,000
Total Liabilities and	
Shareholders' Equity	$598,000

8

BALANCE SHEET RATIOS

Although financial statements provide much useful information, the large numbers they often contain and the varying sizes of companies make it difficult to compare performance from company to company and from year to year within one company. Ratio analysis is a useful technique for evaluating the various financial characteristics of a company. A ratio simply defines a relationship between two numbers; applying ratio analysis to financial statements enables you to make judgments about the success, failure, and progress of a company over time and to evaluate how a company is performing compared with similar companies in the same industry. Most industry and trade associations publish industry average ratios based on data compiled by the association from reports submitted by its members. Several years' ratios should be compared to determine if any unfavorable trends are developing.

Balance sheet ratios measure *liquidity* (the ability of a firm to meet its current debts) and *leverage* (the extent to which the company is dependent upon the financing of creditors). The three principal measures of liquidity are calculated as follows:

1. Current Ratio $= \dfrac{\text{Current Assets}}{\text{Current Liabilities}}$

This ratio measures the extent to which current assets are available to meet the payment schedule of a company's debts. Whether a specific current ratio is adequate depends on the nature of the business and the characteristics of its assets and liabilities. Although a minimum acceptable current ratio might appear to be 1:1, this ratio provides no margin of safety for inventory shrinkage or uncollectible accounts receivable.

2. Acid-test (or Quick) Ratio =

$$\frac{Cash + Temporary\ Investments + Accounts\ Receivable}{Total\ Current\ Liabilities}$$

The acid-test ratio focuses on the most liquid assets by excluding inventories. This ratio measures the firm's ability to meet its current obligations even if none of the inventory can be sold.

3. Working Capital =
Current Assets − Current Liabilities

This ratio is another way to look at the relationship between current assets and current liabilities. Most financially healthy businesses have positive working capital. Minimum working capital requirements are often stipulated in loan agreements.

Financial leverage refers to the use of debt to finance the assets of a company. Leverage adds risk to the operation of the firm; if a firm does not generate enough revenues to pay the interest on its debt, its creditors can force it into bankruptcy. Two widely used financial leverage ratios are the debt ratio and the debt/equity ratio. Each of the ratios deals with the relationship between debt and equity. The debt ratio is the ratio of total liabilities to total liabilities and owners' equity, whereas the debt/equity ratio is the ratio of total liabilities to total owners' equity. A debt ratio of 50 percent is equivalent to a debt/equity ratio of 1. To illustrate, suppose a firm has the following capital structure:

Liabilities	$120,000
Owners' Equity	360,000
Total Liabilities and Owners' Equity	$480,000

$$\text{Debt Ratio} = \frac{\text{Total liabilities}}{\text{Total liabilities and owners' equity}}$$

$$= \frac{\$120,000}{\$480,000}$$

$$= 25\%$$

$$\text{Debt/Equity Ratio} = \frac{\text{Total liabilities}}{\text{Total owners' equity}}$$

$$= \frac{\$120,000}{\$360,000}$$

$$= 33\frac{1}{3}\%$$

These ratios indicate to creditors how well protected they are in the event the firm becomes insolvent. A high ratio has a negative influence on a company's ability to obtain additional financing. Most nonfinancial firms have a debt ratio below 50 percent, the equivalent of a debt/equity ratio of less than 1, because of the risk associated with a higher proportion of debt in the capital structure.

9

THE INCOME
STATEMENT

The income statement, sometimes called the statement of earnings or the profit-and-loss statement, measures a company's revenues, expenses, and resulting net income over a specified period of time. In contrast, the balance sheet measures the company's financial condition at a specific point in time. While the balance sheet discloses a company's position at the end of the accounting period, the income statement helps readers understand why its financial position changed during the accounting period. Both reports are necessary for an understanding of the operation of the business.

There is no rigid format governing income statements, and it may be tailored to fit the activities of a particular company. However, there are several categories that appear in most financial statements.

Sales of products and services provide the bulk of revenues for most firms. Net sales (the amount of sales originally recorded less the value of merchandise subsequently returned by customers) is used to record sales, sometimes called sales revenue or simply revenue (see Exhibit 4).

Cost of goods sold is the cost of the inventory or goods sold to customers. This is shown as an expense item on the income statement and is usually the largest of all the expenses incurred by a firm. Cost of goods sold is calculated by adding purchases to beginning inventory and subtracting ending inventory.

COST OF GOODS SOLD

Beginning Inventory	$ 5,000
Purchases	30,000
Goods Available for Sale	35,000
Ending Inventory	(10,000)
Cost of Goods Sold	$25,000

Gross profit (or gross margin) is the difference between sales and cost of goods sold. It is often expressed as a percentage of sales, as well as in dollar amounts. The percentage gross profit (gross profit/sales) is a very significant number, because it indicates the average markup on the merchandise sold. A manager who knows his or her gross profit percentage can calculate the markup necessary to obtain the gross profit needed for a profitable operation.

Selling, general, and administrative expenses are the operating expenses of the company and include such expenses as salaries and wages, depreciation, utilities, supplies, taxes, bad debts, advertising, insurance, and freight. In Exhibit 4, all these expenses are lumped together, but some income statements report separately on each of the operating expense categories.

Net income from operations or operating income is one of the most important measures of a company's performance. It indicates how successful the company has been in generating profit from its principal operations.

Interest expense is the cost of using borrowed funds. This expense is reported separately from operating expenses, because it is a function of how assets are financed rather than how they are used.

Income tax is shown after all the other expenses have been deducted, because it is a function of the company's income before taxes.

Earnings (or net income) per share of common stock outstanding is always reported at the bottom of a corporation's income statement. This figure, which receives a great deal of attention in the financial markets, is a key factor in determining the market price of a company's common stock. It is discussed in greater detail in Key 30.

EXHIBIT 4

DUGAN TOOLS, INC.
Income Statement
For the Year Ending December 31, 1991

Net sales	$3,5000,000
Cost of goods sold	2,650,000
Gross profit	850,000
Selling, general, and administrative expenses	540,000
Net income from operation	310,000
Interest expense	40,000
Income before taxes	270,000
Income taxes	90,000
Net income	180,000
Earning per common share outstanding	$.36

10

INCOME STATEMENT RATIOS

In contrast to the snapshot concept of the balance sheet, which captures a company's position as of a given date, the income statement indicates the flow of sales, expenses, and earnings during a period of time. It provides an indication of how well the company operated during the accounting period.

Analysts employ financial ratios because numbers in isolation have little value. The knowledge that net income is $1 million is more informative if it can be compared against the sales figure that produced this income and the assets or owners' equity available to the firm.

Financial ratios are particularly useful for analyzing a company's performance relative to its industry. The influence of industry-wide conditions on the businesses within the industry is always strong. Consequently, analysis of an individual business without consideration of industry trends is meaningless. Comparative financial information can be obtained from the following books:

Almanac of Business and Industrial Financial Ratios, Leo Troy, Prentice-Hall, Inc., Englewood Cliffs, NJ 07632

Annual Statement Studies, Robert Morris Associates, P.O. Box 8500, s-1140, Philadelphia, PA 19178

Key Business Ratios, Dun & Bradstreet, Inc., Public Relations and Advertising Department, 99 Church Street, New York, NY 10007

The most prominent financial-statement ratio is earnings per share. Because it is the most widely publicized product of the accounting process, it will be discussed in

Key 30. Other useful financial statement ratios include the following:

$$1. \text{ Gross Profit Margin } = \frac{\text{Gross Profit}}{\text{Net Sales}}$$

Gross profit margin is a measure of a company's ability to meet its selling, general, and administrative expenses and to earn a profit. Changes in this ratio may indicate changes in sales prices, changes in unit costs for goods purchased, or changes in the sales mix (the quantity of goods with low profit margins that is sold compared to the quantity of goods with high profit margins sold). Trends in a company's gross profit margin are significant, as is a comparison of a company's gross profit margin with that of other businesses in the industry.

$$2. \text{ Operating Profit Margin } = \frac{\text{Operating Profit}}{\text{Net Sales}}$$

Operating profit is also known as net income from operations and operating income. This ratio is an extremely important measure of management's ability to control operating costs and raise productivity. Operating income is profit from continuing operations before depreciation, interest, taxes, and irregular gains and losses. A company's operating margin is often a better measure of management skill than is its net profit margin.

$$3. \text{ Net Profit Margin } = \frac{\text{Net Profit Before Tax}}{\text{Net Sales}}$$

Net profit margin is calculated before deducting income tax because tax rates and tax liabilities vary among companies for many reasons, making comparisons after taxes more difficult to interpret. This ratio enables you to compare a company's return on sales with the performance of other companies in the industry.

11

STATEMENT OF CASH FLOWS

Most users of financial statements agree that the income statement and the balance sheet disclose valuable information to managers, investors, creditors, and other interested parties. Yet, despite their usefulness, these financial statements have a serious deficiency—namely, the inability to disclose the specific events and transactions that occurred during an accounting period. For example, consider the sale of a machine. The income statement reveals the gain or loss associated with its sale; however, the cost of the machine and the cash received from its sale cannot be gleaned from either the balance sheet or the income statement. The cash received is included in the cash account, which reflects *all* activities that involve the inflow and outflow of cash. The original cost of the machine is obscured by other cash transactions for machinery, all of which are disclosed as a single balance sheet item called machinery. Although a comparison of the beginning and ending balances of cash and machinery reveals changes in the amounts of these items, the actual transaction is difficult to detect because of all the other transactions that also affect these accounts.

The purpose of the statement of cash flows is to identify the sources and uses of cash during the accounting period. To do this, the statement divides a business's operations into the three main activity groups that cause assets to change: operating, investing, and financing activities (see Exhibit 5 at the end of this key). The information contained on the statement is helpful in answering questions such as the following:

1. Why does net income differ from the associated cash receipts and payments?
2. Did the company's cash result from operations, sale of assets, bank loans, or investments by owners?
3. Is the cash generated from the company's operations sufficient to continue paying the dividend?
4. Did the company use its cash to buy new assets? Reduce debt? Pay dividends?

By presenting information on how cash is obtained and used by a business, the statement of cash flows provides insight into transactions and events that cannot be obtained by examining the other financial statements. Note that in Exhibit 5 the effects of individual transactions are disclosed under investing and financing activities.

The first activity disclosed in the statement is operating activities. Using net income as the starting point for this measure of cash changes indicates the direct link between the income statement and the statement of cash flows. Note that net income is adjusted for items affecting net income but not affecting cash.

Most expenses involve a corresponding outflow of cash. Depreciation, however, although it is deducted as an expense from net income, does not require the use of cash. Recall that depreciation is the process of recognizing part of the cost of an asset as an expense each year over its useful life. Since depreciation is a noncash reduction in net income, it is added back to determine cash flow from operations.

Changes in the balances of current accounts other than cash also have implications for cash flow. The increase in accounts receivable is subtracted from net income because the increase results from sales included in net income that have not yet been collected in cash. (Recall that accounts receivable is the sales of goods and services on credit.) In addition, the increase in merchandise inventory is deducted because cash was spent to acquire the additional inventory. As a rule, decreases in current assets other than cash and increases in current liabilities are added back to net income, whereas increases in current assets and decreases in current liabilities are subtracted.

Investing activities involve changes in a firm's long-term investments and property, plant, and equipment. Exhibit 5 reveals that machinery was sold for $80,000.

Financing activities involve liabilities and stockholders' equity items, including amounts raised from the sale of long-term debt and common stock and dividends paid on common stock. Items such as stocks, bonds, and loans provide a business with cash inflows and commit it to eventual cash outflows (e.g., dividends and repayment of principal). Transactions involving long-term debt and common stock are illustrated in Exhibit 5.

The net increase shown at the bottom of Exhibit 5 is the change in the cash balance from the beginning to the end of the accounting period. The statement of cash flows shows why the cash balance changed by $555,000 during the accounting period.

EXHIBIT 5

ROBBINS MACHINE SHOP, INC.
Statement of Cash Flows
For the Year Ending December 31, 1991

Cash flows from operating activities:	
Net income	$185,000
Add (deduct) items not affecting cash:	
Depreciation expense	20,000
Increase in accounts receivable	(250,000)
Increase in merchandise inventory	(110,000)
Net cash used by operating activities	(155,000)
Cash flows from investing activities:	
Cash received from sale of machine	80,000
Cash flows from financing activities:	
Cash received from sale of long-term debt	50,000
Cash received from sale of common stock	500,000
Payment of cash dividend on common stock	80,000
Net cash provided by financing activities	630,000
Net increase in cash this year	$555,000

12

MANAGEMENT RATIOS

Management ratios are extremely important in evaluating management performance. Usually, they are derived from both the balance sheet and the income statement. Some of these ratios evaluate how effectively certain assets are turned into cash and provide information on how efficiently the enterprise uses its assets. Other management ratios assist in evaluating how well the company has operated during the year. These ratios are computed on the basis of sales or by using an investment base such as total assets or common stockholders' equity. The following are some of the key management ratios:

1. $\text{Inventory Turnover} = \dfrac{\text{Costs of goods sold}}{\text{Average inventory at cost}}$

The inventory turnover ratio measures how rapidly inventory is sold. The inventory turnover divided by 365 indicates the average number of days it takes to sell inventory. Generally speaking, the higher the inventory turnover, the more profitable the enterprise. This ratio can provide clues to the salability of inventory and whether pricing problems exist.

2. $\text{Accounts receivable turnover} = \dfrac{\text{Credit Sales}}{\text{Average Accounts Receivable}}$

This ratio provides an indicator of how successfully a company collects its receivables. Receivables should be collected in accordance with their terms. If a company is slow in converting its receivables into cash, its liquidity may be seriously undermined.

3. Rate of return on assets $= \dfrac{\text{Net Profit Before Tax}}{\text{Total Assets}}$

This ratio measures how efficiently profits are being generated from the business's assets. The best comparison is with the ratios of companies in a similar business or industry. A ratio that is low compared with industry averages indicates that business assets are being used inefficiently.

4. Rate of return on common stock equity $= \dfrac{\text{Net income } - \text{ preferred dividends}}{\text{Common stockholders' equity}}$

This ratio gives the percentage return on funds invested in the business by its owners. If the ROE is less than the rate of return on a relatively risk-free investment, such as a money-market fund or savings account, the owner may be wise to sell his or her interest in the company.

13

STATEMENT OF RETAINED EARNINGS

A financial statement called the statement of retained earnings is often included with the income statement, balance sheet, and statement of cash flows in a company's financial statements. The statement of retained earnings explains any changes in the balance of the retained earnings account during the accounting period and relates the income statement to the balance sheet. The statement can be divided into three sections:

1. **Prior-Period Adjustments.** Prior-period adjustments are necessary when a company has incorrectly recorded an item in a prior accounting period. For example, suppose a company determines that it overstated depreciation in a prior period, making both the income statement and the tax return for the period incorrect. Such errors are corrected in the statement of retained earnings and not the income statement. Thus, they do not enter into the calculation of net income at all but are included in the statement of retained earnings. (See Exhibit 6.)

2. **Net Income.** The net income figure on the statement of retained earnings is the same number reported in the income statement. If the company incurred a loss in the accounting period being covered, the loss is deducted from retained earnings.

3. **Dividends.** Dividends represent distribution to stockholders in the form of cash, other assets, or the company's own stock. Usually, only a portion of the income earned in a year is paid out in dividends. The

portion not paid out, i.e., retained earnings, is invested in the business to finance future expansion.

Some companies combine the income statement and the retained earnings statement in a single statement. The principal advantage of combining the two statements is that all items affecting income appear on a single statement. Some accountants object to this approach because it deemphasizes net income by not placing this figure at the bottom of the statement. An example of a partial combined income statement and retained earnings is presented below.

DEIS COMPANY
Combined Income Statement and Retained Earnings
(lower portion only)

Net income for the year	$ 780,000
Retained earnings at the beginning of the year	1,750,000
Less: Cash dividends declared and paid	250,000
Retained earnings at the end of the year	$2,280,000

EXHIBIT 6

STRAWSER BOOKS, INC.
Retained Earnings Statement
For Year Ending December 31, 1991

Net income		$3,250,000
Add: Retained earnings, Jan. 1, 1991,		
as previously reported	$1,400,000	
Less: Prior period adjustment—		
overstatement of depreciation		
in 1990 due, less applicable		
income tax effect of $100,000	200,000	
Retained earnings, Jan. 1, 1991 as restated		1,600,000
Deduct dividends declared on common		
stock, at $3 per share		1,400,000
Retained earnings December 31, 1991		$3,450,000

14

TEMPORARY INVESTMENTS

Investments are classified as either temporary (current assets) or long-term (noncurrent assets). An investment is classified as a temporary investment if two criteria are met:

1. The investment is readily marketable (easily sold at the current price).
2. It is management's intention to convert the investment into cash as needed within one year.

If these criteria are not met, the investment is classified as a long-term investment and is then disclosed on the balance sheet between current assets and property, plant, and equipment.

Temporary investments (also called marketable securities) consist of the following:

- **Short-term paper**—certificates of deposit and U.S. Treasury bills
- **Marketable debt securities**—government and corporate bonds
- **Marketable equity securities**—preferred or common stock of other companies

Investments are recorded at cost when acquired. Cost includes the acquisition price plus the incidental costs incurred in purchasing the investment, such as brokerage fees and taxes. Subsequent to acquisition, evaluation varies depending upon the type of investment. Short-term paper should continue to be valued at cost, marketable equity securities at the lower of cost or market, and marketable debt securities at cost or the lower of cost or market.

41

Marketable equity securities are any equity securities for which quotations are available from a national or over-the-counter market. Examples include common stock and preferred stock, as well as the right to acquire or dispose of such shares (e.g., warrants, rights, and options). Marketable equity securities should be accounted for by using the lower of aggregate cost or market value at the balance-sheet date; that is, the investment is recorded at its original cost unless the current market value is lower. To apply this rule, the aggregate cost of the portfolio is compared with the aggregate market value of the portfolio. If aggregate cost exceeds aggregate market value, the investments are shown on the balance sheet at their aggregate market value and a loss is reported in the income statement for the period. Note that this approach calls for a loss to be reported as a result of the decline in the market value of the entire portfolio, not of a specific security.

For example, consider a portfolio that consists of two stocks: ABC Company and XYZ Company. Suppose ABC Company stock originally cost $40 per share and currently sells for $55, while XYZ stock originally cost $105 and now sells for $70. We would group these stocks into a portfolio and compare their total cost to their total market value. In this case, the portfolio cost $145 ($40 + $105) and the current market value is $125 ($55 + $70). Because current market value is $20 less than original or historical cost ($145 − $125), we write the portfolio down in value by $20 and report it on the balance sheet at $125. The write-down of $20 is an unrealized loss that is reported in the income statement for the period.

In subsequent periods, recoveries of market value are recognized to the extent that the market value of the portfolio does not exceed original cost. Unrealized gains above historical or original cost are not recognized in determining income. In this case, accountants recognize a loss before the actual sale of securities but do not recognize any gain until the securities are sold.

Temporary investments can be added to cash and cash equivalents to give analysts the current overall cash position of the company. Remember that by definition temporary investments are easily convertible into cash; therefore, considering them the equivalent of cash is normally justifiable.

15

ACCOUNTS RECEIVABLE

Accounts receivable result from the sale of goods and services. They are unwritten promises by customers to pay the amount due within a specified time period (normally 30 to 60 days). Because receivables are expected to be collected within a short period of time, they are classified on the balance sheet as current assets. Generally accepted accounting principles (GAAP) require accounts receivable to be disclosed at their net realizable value; the amount of cash the company expects to realize or collect from the receivable. This figure equals the gross amount of the receivable less the amount that is estimated to be uncollectible. Thus, if at the end of an accounting period a company has accounts receivable of $100,000 of which it estimates that $2,000 will be uncollectible, the net realizable value is $98,000.

Accounts receivable and the accompanying revenue should be recognized by the seller on the date of sale. The amount of revenue and related receivable to be recognized is usually the agreed-upon exchange price between the two parties.

Trade discounts are percentage reductions in quoted list prices granted for volume purchases, different classes of buyers, and quick sales. Trade discounts are not recognized for financial accounting purposes; instead, they are always deducted prior to recording the accounts receivable arising from a credit sales transaction.

Sellers offer cash discounts as an inducement for prompt payment and to reduce the risk of nonpayment by customers. For example, assume a $100 sale on credit on July 1 has terms of 2/10, n/30. The buyer has the option of paying $98 ($100 − [.02 × 100]) by July 11 or paying $100 on July 31. Cash discounts are recognized in the accounts when payment is received, and the sales discounts balance is deducted from sales in the income statement to arrive at net sales.

The computation of net realizable value, requires a provision for uncollectible amounts or bad debts. The lost revenue is reflected in the financial statements as a decrease in the current asset (accounts receivable) and an accompanying decrease in net income and owners' or stockholders' equity.

Each year the asset side of the balance sheet includes an item called "allowance for doubtful accounts" or "allowance for bad debts." This amount is subtracted from accounts receivable on the balance sheet to arrive at the net amount (net realizable value) of accounts receivable. Because it is deducted in the asset section, allowance for doubtful accounts is called a *contra-asset account*—an item subtracted from an asset to determine its value on the balance sheet. Accounts receivable appears as follows on the balance sheet:

Accounts receivable	$100,000
Less: Allowance for bad debts	(5,000)
Net accounts receivable	$ 95,000

Different approaches may be used in estimating the uncollectibles. Using past experience, a firm can estimate a statistical relationship between its year-end balance of accounts receivable and its expected bad debt and then assign to an allowance account an amount equal to an appropriate percentage of the year-end receivables.

A more realistic and widely used approach is to age the receivables. Under this approach, different percentages are assigned to the various age categories of accounts receivable based upon past experience. The following schedule is a simple example:

Accounts Receivable
Aging Schedule

Age	Amount	Percentage Estimated Uncollectible	Required Allowance Balance
Current	$180,000	3%	$5,400
31–60 days	64,000	10%	6,400
61–90 days	30,000	15%	4,500
91–120 days	24,000	25%	6,000
Over 120 days	10,000	40%	4,000
Totals	$308,000		$26,300

The amount of $26,300 would thus be the desired balance in the allowance account at the balance sheet date. If the company decides that an individual account is uncollectible, it writes off the amount and charges it to the allowance for bad debts account. Charging off the accounts assumed to be uncollectible reduces the balance in the allowance account. At the end of the year, the allowance account is adjusted to bring it up to the expected loss amount. All additions to update the allowance account are charged to the "bad debt expense" account and deducted on the income statement.

The ratio of accounts receivable to sales can be an important indicator of possible financial difficulty. The balance in a company's accounts receivable should be at a level that is normal for its industry; for example, in the casino equipment industry, receivables of up to 25 percent of annual sales are considered acceptable.

In evaluating the ratio of accounts receivable to sales, it is important to analyze changes over time. An increase in the ratio can raise some troubling questions. Is credit too loose, causing increased returns and delinquencies? Is collection lax? Are customers dissatisfied with the product or service and therefore withholding payment?

16

INVENTORY

Inventories are the most significant current asset of many businesses. They are usually carried (valued) at cost or the lower of cost or market (the cost to replace the item either through purchase or through manufacture) on the balance sheet. If the cost of replacing the item is less than the cost of acquiring or manufacturing it, the lower amount is used in valuing inventories. For example, suppose the lower of cost or market method is used to value inventory consisting of 100 items whose original cost was $5 apiece. If the current cost of replacing these items is $4.50, the inventory will be valued on the balance sheet at $45 (100 × $4.50 per item).

The valuation of inventories can be confusing, because even the determination of cost can involve the choice of one of several different alternatives. Common sense tells us that cost is simply the original purchase price of an item, but its actual determination is considerably more complicated. With companies acquiring many units of inventory (sometimes millions of items), it is not practical to attempt to identify the actual cost of a particular item every time an item is sold from inventory. Instead, three alternatives or cost-flow assumptions are widely used in valuing inventory: weighted average, first-in first-out (FIFO); and last-in, first-out (LIFO).

The *weighted-average method* requires determining the total cost of all goods available for sale during the period and dividing by the number of units available for sale. The average unit cost is then used to value ending inventory and cost of goods sold. For Thibodeaux Toys

Company, the average cost per unit is determined as follows:

Cost of goods available	$434,500
Units available	80
Average cost per unit ($323,500/80)	$4043.75

This average cost is then used to compute ending inventory and cost of goods sold:

Cost of goods available (80 units)	$323,500.00
Less ending inventory	
10 boats at $4043.75	40,437.50
Cost of goods sold (70 units at $4043.75)	$283,062.50

Example:

Thibodeaux Boats Company
1991

	Units	Unit Cost	Total Cost
Beginning inventory	10	$3,000	$30,000
2-1-90	25	4,000	100,000
7-1-90	30	4,200	126,000
12-1-90	15	4,500	67,500
Total boats available to sell	80		$323,500
Number of boats sold	70		
Ending inventory	10		

Under first-in, first-out, the costs of the earliest purchases are assigned to cost of goods sold and the costs of the most recent purchases are allocated to ending inventory. This assumption of cost flow usually conforms to the physical flow of goods. Using FIFO, the ten units in ending inventory are assumed to consist of those purchased on 12-1-90: ten units at $4,500 each equal $45,000. The cost of goods sold can be computed as follows:

Cost of goods available (80 units)	$323,500
Less ending inventory (10 units)	(45,000)
Cost of goods sold (70 units)	$278,500

The last-in, first-out method assigns costs of the latest purchases to cost of goods sold and allocates the oldest costs to ending inventory. LIFO seldom conforms to the actual physical flow of goods.

In our example, the ten units in inventory are assigned a cost of $3,000 each for a total of $30,000. Cost of goods sold is computed below:

Cost of goods available (80 units)	$323,500
Less ending inventory (10 units)	30,000
Cost of goods sold (70 units)	$293,500

When inventory costs are rising, as in inflationary periods, LIFO results in a higher balance for inventory on the balance sheet, a lower cost of goods sold on the income statement, and therefore greater net income. This difference occurs because the LIFO assumption results in the transfer of the more recent, higher costs to cost of goods sold and the allocation of earlier, lower costs to the inventory balance shown on the income statement.

Note that in our illustration inventory costs are rising throughout the period and cost of goods sold and ending inventory under FIFO are, respectively, $278,500 and $45,000 whereas cost of goods sold and ending inventory under LIFO are $293,500 and $30,000. The choice of inventory costing assumption can significantly affect both the balance sheet and the income statement.

During the late 1970s, when inflation reached double digits, the higher net income produced under the FIFO assumption resulted in higher income taxes for many companies than if current costs had been recognized under LIFO. (Because taxes must be paid on these profits and the cost of replacing the inventory sold is considerably higher than historical cost during a period of high inflation, financial statements about the company's real (adjusted for inflation) profitability can be misleading.) Many companies decided to change from FIFO to LIFO even though the adoption of LIFO would reduce the reported amount of net income on their income statements (the IRS requires that LIFO be used for financial accounting purposes if it is adopted for tax purposes) because reducing net income enabled them to pay lower taxes.

17

INTANGIBLE ASSETS

Intangible assets are conferred rights that lack physical substance but possess economic value. For the following reasons, the value of intangible assets is generally more uncertain than that of tangible assets:
- The value may be higher dependent upon competitive conditions.
- The value may exist only for a particular organization.
- The asset may have an indeterminate life.

Copyrights, trademarks and trade names, licenses, franchises, and goodwill are examples of intangible assets. All intangible assets are recorded at cost—that is, the total of purchase cost plus expenditures necessary to make the intangible asset ready for use. Only out-of-pocket costs, such as legal fees and application and filing fees, are recorded as costs of developing specific intangible assets such as patents. The basic costs of development, which are similar to research and development, are recognized as expenses when incurred.

All intangible assets must be amortized over their useful lives, which in no case should exceed forty years. The term "amortization" has essentially the same meaning as depreciation, except that amortization is used in discussing intangible assets and depreciation is used in discussing tangible assets. Amortization is the expensing of a portion of the cost of the asset each year. Thus, for an intangible asset costing $10,000 and having an estimated useful life of ten years, a business recognizes $1,000 of amortization expense each year on the income statement and the value of the asset is reduced each year by $1,000 on the balance sheet.

For many years, research and development (R&D) costs were recognized as intangible assets. Problems arose because most R&D efforts have uncertain benefits and are difficult to assign to future periods. In addition, companies varied in their policies regarding the costs that should be recognized as assets because they provide future benefits and the costs that should be expensed immediately because they do not provide future benefits. In an effort to enhance comparability and reduce the possibility of income manipulation, a rule was passed stipulating that all research and development costs be charged to expense in the period incurred.

Certain intangibles that lack specific identifiability—such as customer loyalty, good management, and advantageous geographical location—are classified as goodwill. Internal expenditures producing goodwill must be expensed; however, purchased goodwill is recognized and recorded as an intangible asset. In other words, goodwill is recorded only when one company buys another. The amount of goodwill to be recognized is measured by the difference between the purchase price of the acquired firm as a whole and the fair market value of its net assets (assets − liabilities). For example, suppose that Corporation A pays $3 million to acquire Corporation B. If the market value of Corporation B's assets is $3.4 million and its liabilities are valued at $900,000, then goodwill will be shown on Corporation A's balance sheet as $500,000 [$3,000,000 − ($3,400,000 − $900,000)].

Users of financial statements should be aware that the amount shown for intangible assets frequently understates the current market value of such assets. Many corporate takeovers in the 1980s were driven by a wish to acquire valuable brandnames. In the last decade, corporations such as the Walt Disney Co. and Coca-Cola have become very successful at exploiting their trademarks. Both of these companies put their names on a multitude of consumer goods unrelated to the products with which they were originally identified. The name Coca-Cola has achieved international recognition and is worth billions to the company. Yet Coca-Cola's 1989 annual report puts the total value of all its intangible assets, including goodwill, at $231 million. This amount dramatically understates the current market value of the intangible assets of Coke.

Alternatively, if a substantial amount is shown for goodwill, the market value of intangible assets may be overstated. Goodwill is the buyer's estimate of the excess of investment value over asset value. However, this estimate reflects projections of earnings under new management; if the company has financial difficulties, the goodwill can evaporate quickly. The value of goodwill is frequently uncertain, and many analysts do not include it in their valuation of a firm.

18

PROPERTY, PLANT, AND EQUIPMENT

Property, plant, and equipment (PP&E) is the long-lived, tangible assets that are used by an organization in the production or sale of inventory or in the provision of goods and services. Examples are land, equipment, buildings, fixtures, and furniture, all of which have productive lives exceeding one year.

PP&E is initially valued at its acquisition cost (all the expenditures necessary to prepare the asset for its intended use). These expenditures include the invoice price of the asset, freight charges, assembly, and costs incurred for installation and testing. It is presented on the balance sheet at book value, which is the asset's total acquisition cost less accumulated depreciation (the total amount of depreciation expense deducted on the income statement since acquisition). All components of PP&E except land are subject to depreciation (the allocation of cost, reduced by the estimate of the salvage value of the asset, to expense over the useful life of the asset). Since depreciation involves a process of cost allocation, it is not a reliable indicator of market value.

Generally accepted accounting principles require that the following information be disclosed either in the body of a financial statement or in the footnotes:
• Total depreciation expense for the period
• Depreciation method or methods used
• Groupings of acquisition costs of fixed assets, classified by nature or by function
• Related groupings of accumulated depreciation for each category of fixed assets

The recorded cost of land includes:
- The purchase price
- The costs of closing the transaction and obtaining title
- The costs of surveys
- The costs of preparing the land for its intended use, such as grading, filling, and clearing
- The costs of land improvements that have an indefinite life

The cost of the removal of old buildings on land purchased for the purpose of constructing a new building is part of land costs, because these costs are necessary to prepare the land for its intended use. Since land has an indefinite economic life, it is not subject to depreciation.

The cost of a building includes:
- The contract price
- The costs of renovation
- The costs of excavation
- The costs of plans, blueprints, and building permits
- Architectural and engineering fees

Unanticipated construction costs, such as a strike or weather damage, are expensed. Property taxes and insurance during construction may be either capitalized (included as part of the cost of the asset) or expensed.

The cost of equipment also includes all expenditures incurred in acquiring the asset and preparing it for its intended use. Some of the costs that should be capitalized in an appropriate asset account include:
- The purchase price
- Freight and handling costs
- Insurance while in transit
- Costs of installation
- Costs of conducting trial runs

When several dissimilar assets categorized as PP&E are acquired for a lump-sum purchase price, the total purchase costs should be allocated among the individual assets in the group based upon their respective market values. If the total market value is greater than the total cost, the cost should be allocated proportionately, according to the following formula:

$$\frac{\text{Fair Market Value of Individual Assets}}{\text{Fair Market Value of Assets Acquired}} \times \text{Total Cost}$$

For example, if three assets that are purchased for a lump sum of $120,000 have fair market values at the time of purchase of $40,000, $50,000, and $70,000, respectively, if purchased separately, the cost is allocated as follows:

Asset A $\quad \dfrac{\$\ 40,000}{160,000} \times 120,000 = \quad \$30,000$

Asset B $\quad \dfrac{50,000}{160,000} \times 120,000 = \quad 37,500$

Asset C $\quad \dfrac{70,000}{160,000} \times 120,000 = \quad \dfrac{52,500}{\$120,000}$

The value of PP&E shown on the balance can be misleading. In view of the effect of inflation on the current cost of PP&E, the amounts shown for old PP&E carried on at actual cost less depreciation are usually much less than the cost of replacing the same equipment with used equipment. This helps to explain the willingness of buyers to pay 1½ to 2 times the book value (assets − liabilities) for an acquired firm.

19

INCOME TAXES

The amount that corporations pay to the Internal Revenue Service almost always differs from the income tax expense deducted in the income statement for the purpose of determining net income. The reason for the disparity is that the accounting methods used to determine the income tax payable to the IRS can differ from those used to determine pretax accounting income in the income statement. In the tax return, taxable income is computed in accordance with prescribed regulations and rules, whereas pretax accounting income is measured in accordance with generally accepted accounting principles (GAAP).

A temporary (or timing) difference between accounting income and taxable income may occur when revenues and expenses are recognized in different accounting periods for income tax and financial reporting purposes. Such a difference may occur, for example, if a company uses an accelerated method of depreciation for a fixed asset when computing its taxes and the straight-line method of depreciation when preparing financial statements. This difference means that depreciation expense will be greater on the tax return than on the books early in the life of the asset; the reverse will be true later in the life of the asset.

A permanent difference in reported income may exist when an item affects either financial income or taxable income, but not both. For example, interest income on municipal bonds is included in accounting income, but it is excluded from taxable income because it is tax exempt. Unlike timing differences, permanent differences do not result in tax consequences and do not affect future accounting periods.

The procedure required to account for income taxes when timing differences exist between financial accounting income and taxable income is known as interperiod tax allocation. Interperiod tax allocation requires that the amount of income tax expense to be recognized on the income statement in a given year be determined by the pretax accounting income recognized that year. However, income tax payable, disclosed on the company's balance sheet, is based on taxable income computed on the tax return for the year. The difference between pretax accounting income and taxable income is multiplied by the tax rate; the result is shown in an account called deferred income taxes; which can be either an asset or a liability. Pretax accounting income usually exceeds taxable income, and therefore the deferred income taxes account is disclosed as a liability.

When a timing difference is identified and measured, companies determine the future year in which the difference will reverse. This procedure, called scheduling, is necessary to determine the amount of deferred taxes to be recognized. For example, suppose that at the beginning of Year 1, an organization buys $100,000 of depreciable assets and uses straight-line depreciation for financial accounting purposes and an accelerated method for tax purposes:

	Amount of Depreciation		Timing Difference	
	Financial Reporting	Tax		
Year	Income	Income	Annual	Cumulative
1	$2,000	$5,000	$3,000	$3,000
2	2,000	3,000	1,000	4,000
3	2,000	2,000	0	4,000
4	2,000	0	(2,000)	2,000
5	2,000	0	(2,000)	0
	$10,000	$10,000	$	

At the end of Year 1, the timing difference is $3,000. If this is the only timing difference for the company, the balance in the deferred income taxes account represents a liability because it is a commitment to pay a future tax. Note that the deferred balance reverses in years 3 and 4, producing a zero balance in the account.

For many companies, the deferred income tax liability grows over time. This occurs because as companies grow, they require increasing amounts of depreciable assets. The timing difference between book and tax depreciation increases each year because the excess of depreciation expense recognized on the income statement over depreciation recognized for tax purposes for older assets is more than offset by the excess of tax depreciation over book depreciation for newer assets.

20

DIVIDENDS

Dividends are distributions to shareholders. Although they usually take the form of cash or stock, dividends can consist of property such as merchandise, real estate, or investments. Typically, corporations can declare dividends only out of earnings, although some state laws and corporate agreements permit the declaration of dividends from sources other than earnings. Dividends based on sources other than earnings are sometimes called "liquidating" dividends, because they are a return of the stockholders' investment rather than of profits.

Cash dividends are the portion of earnings or profits distributed to stockholders as cash. They become a liability of the corporation after the board of directors properly approves their future payment. Cash dividends are usually paid on a quarterly basis shortly after the dividend resolution has been approved by the board of directors. Dividends cannot be paid immediately, because the ongoing purchase and sale of the corporation's stock require that a current list of stockholders be prepared.

For example, a resolution approved at the April 10 (declaration date) meeting of the board of directors might be declared payable on May 5 (payment date) to all stockholders of record as of April 25 (record date). The provision of a two-week grace period from April 10 to April 25 allows any transfers in process to be completed and registered with the transfer agent; dividends are payable only to stockholders of record as of the record date (in this case, April 25), and anyone owning the stock as of April 25 receives the dividend even if the stock is sold between April 25 and the date of payment, May 5. On the day after the record date, the stock usually falls slightly in price to compensate for the fact that it no longer qualifies for the latest dividend (called trading ex-dividend).

The *payout ratio* is the ratio of cash dividends to net income. In other words, it is the percentage of net income or earnings that the corporation's board of directors pays out in cash. Although about 60 percent of the average corporation's earnings is paid out in the form of cash dividends, the percentage payout can vary widely. Small, high-growth companies tend to have lower payout ratios than mature companies, because their need to reinvest the cash generated from operations in capital facilities to finance future growth is stronger than that of mature, low-growth companies.

The *dividend yield percentage,* obtained by dividing the annual cash dividend by the closing price of the stock, is often reported in the stock tables of major newspapers. The annual cash dividend is based on the rate of the last quarterly payout. If the dividend in the last quarter was $.25 per share, the annual dividend is assumed to be $1.00. This number can be compared with the yield of other stocks and with the interest paid on debt instruments.

A *stock split* is the issuance to stockholders of new shares of stock; a 2-for-1 split, for example, gives each stockholder two new shares for each old share. A *stock dividend* is simply a small stock split. For example, if a corporation issues a 5-percent stock dividend, the owner of 100 shares receives an additional five shares of stock. Essentially, all that happens is that the total number of shares outstanding increases, the price per share decreases proportionately, and the total value of the owners' common stock remains unchanged. If nothing is gained through stock dividends or stock splits, why do companies issue them? One reason is to maintain an attractive price for a stock. An unsupported tradition on Wall Street is that an absolute stock price of between

$25 and $50 is most appealing to investors; if a stock's price is getting too high to attract investors, the company may declare a stock split, effectively cutting the price. Also, stockholders seem to react positively to distributions of additional shares even if the total value of their holdings remains unchanged; corporations often issue stock dividends when cash dividends are unaffordable.

21

CONTINGENT LIABILITIES

Contingencies are defined as existing conditions that will be resolved by the occurrence of future events and that may result in gain (gain contingency) or loss (loss contingency). A liability that results from a loss contingency is called a contingent liability. Contingent liabilities (e.g., lawsuits) are obligations that may exist depending on the outcome of uncertain future events. If an organization believes that a contingent liability exists and if the amount of the liability can be estimated, the contingent liability should be reflected in the financial statements.

The accounting problems related to contingent liabilities center around the following issues:
• When should the effects of a contingency be recorded in the financial statements?
• If contingencies are not reflected in the financial statements, what disclosures, if any, should be made in the footnotes to the financial statements?

According to generally accepted accounting principles, a loss contingency should be accrued (recognized in the financial statements) by a charge against earnings if it is probable that an asset has been impaired or a liability incurred at the balance sheet date (implying that a future event confirming the loss will take place) and if the loss can be reasonably estimated.

GAAP provides the following definitions of three points on the range of probability:
  1. **Probable**—the future event or events are likely to occur.
  2. **Reasonably possible**—the chance of the future

event or events occurring is more than remote (slight) but less than likely (probable).

3. **Remote**—the chance of the future event or events occurring is slight.

The interpretation of such terms as "probable," "reasonably possible," and "remote" varies significantly between firms; as a result, disclosure by different firms concerning contingencies can vary in nature and extent. The following items are examples of loss contingencies:

- Collectibility of receivables
- Obligations related to product warranties and product defects
- Risk of loss or damage of property by fire, explosion, or other hazards
- Threat of expropriation of assets
- Pending or threatened litigation
- Actual or possible claims and assessments
- Risk of loss from catastrophes assumed by property and casualty insurance firms
- Guarantees of indebtedness of others

No recognition in the financial statements is made for a loss contingency unless the loss is both probable and estimable. However, if these two conditions have not been met but it is reasonably possible that a loss has been incurred, that loss contingency should be disclosed as a footnote to the financial statements and should include the nature of the contingency and either an estimate of the possible loss or range of loss or a statement that an estimate cannot be made.

Losses that are usually accrued include uncollectible receivables and obligations related to premium offers, product warranties, and product defects. Loss contingencies that may be accrued if they satisfy the two criteria include the threat of expropriation of assets, actual or possible claims and assessments, pending or threatened litigation, and guarantees of indebtedness of others. Loss contingencies that are usually not accrued include risk of loss or damage from fire or other hazards, general or unspecified business risks, and risk of loss from catastrophes assumed by property and casualty insurance organizations.

Examples of gain contingencies are possible refunds from the government as a result of a tax dispute and pending litigation in which the probable outcome is favorable. Accountants are very conservative in their recognition of gain contingencies. Gain contingencies are never accrued in the financial statement; in addition, they are disclosed in footnotes to the financial statements only when it is probable that a gain contingency will have a favorable outcome.

Most contingencies, if they materialize, have a negative impact on the financial position of the firm or its results of operations. Contingencies that are not reflected in the financial statements (i.e., disclosed in the footnotes) require careful analysis. If the event or events does occur, how severe will the loss be? Will it significantly reduce the firm's available cash? Will it require the company to assume significant additional debt?

22

CORPORATE BONDS

Corporate bonds are long-term debt obligations that are secured by specific assets or by the corporation's promise to repay the amount due. In effect, a bond investor lends money to the bond issuer, and, in return, the issuer promises to pay interest and to repay the principal at maturity.

Because bondholders are creditors, they rank ahead of preferred and common stockholders as claimants to the earnings and assets of the issuing corporation. Interest must be paid to bondholders before dividends can be distributed to stockholders; if the company is dissolved or goes bankrupt, bondholders have a prior claim on assets.

Corporate bonds are usually issued in denominations of $1,000 (the face or maturity value of the bond). The corporation promises to pay interest on the face value, generally semiannually, at a specified annual rate. Thus, a corporation that issues bonds with a face value of $1 million and promises to pay 8 percent yearly interest will pay $40,000 (.08 × $1,000,000 × 6/12) every six months to its bondholders. The specified annual rate of interest is commonly called the coupon rate of interest; in this example, the coupon rate of interest is 8 percent.

Corporations issue the following types of corporate bonds:

• **Debentures**—the most common type of corporate bond. Investors who purchase debentures are general creditors of the corporation, and their investment is protected by the overall assets of the enterprise rather than by any specific assets; debentures are secured by all unpledged corporate assets and property. In general, only financially strong corporations with excellent credit are able to sell debentures.

When a company has more than one bond issue outstanding, the seniority of the issues is often predesignated. A senior issue has a prior claim on interest and repayment of principal over a subordinated bond. This designation becomes significant if serious financial difficulties or bankruptcy threaten the company.

• **First mortgage bonds**—a form of bond secured by specific corporate assets. A bond issuer who is unable to sell debentures or who wishes to add additional security to a new bond issue can designate particular corporate property as collateral for the bond issue; if the company defaults on payments, the bondholders have a claim against the assets pledged. Such a provision may result in a slightly lower coupon rate for the bond.

• **Equipment trust certificate**—a form of bond issued by airlines, railroads, and shipping companies to finance the purchase of new equipment. The certificate gives bondholders first right to the transportation equipment in the event that the interest and principal are not paid. These bonds tend to be very safe since the collateral behind those certificates is readily salable to another transportation company.

• **Income bonds**—bonds are given in exchange for other bonds that have already been issued. These bonds are usually issued only in the case of impending bankruptcy, and interest is payable only if the corporation operates at a profit.

One of the footnotes at the end of each company's financial statements discusses long-term debt, including corporate bonds, that includes interest that the company must pay, and the dates when the debt is due.

23

PENSION PLANS

A pension plan is an agreement under which an employer provides benefits (payments) to employees after they retire. Pensions represent a large and increasing share of total corporate expense, and corporate pension obligations are significant compared to other forms of debt. Pension plans can be divided into two basic types: defined contribution and defined benefit plans.

Under a defined contribution plan, the employer agrees to contribute a certain sum to the fund each period, based upon a formula. The plan specifies the amount to be contributed by the employer rather than the benefits to be received by the employee. An employer who has paid the defined contribution faces no additional liability to provide pension benefits; the amount of an employee's benefits, when he or she becomes eligible to receive them, is usually based upon the amount credited to his or her individual account.

All but a small minority of U.S. organizations use defined benefit plans, in which the benefits to be received upon retirement are determined by a formula that incorporates factors such as the employee's age, years of service, and salary level. The employer's annual contribution to the plan is determined by an actuarial valuation.

Defined benefit plans define the amount and timing of benefits retiring employees will receive, the point at which employees have an irrevocable right to the plan's benefits (become vested), and the funding of the plan. The pension expense to be recorded is based upon estimates of the cost of providing the future benefits. Because so many variables must be estimated to determine the employer's contribution and the expense to be recognized in the determination of net income, accounting and reporting for defined benefit plans are much more complex than they are for defined contribution plans.

Under defined benefit plans, employers are at investment risk because they must make contributions sufficient to meet the cost of the benefits defined in the pension plan. Employees are not at risk, since their pension benefits are determined by a formula rather than by the amount of the employer's contributions. Under a defined contribution plan, however, the employees are at risk because their pension benefits are determined by the amount accumulated in the pension fund.

A funded pension plan is one in which the employer's contributions have been passed on to an independent trustee for the pension plan. If the funds are under the control of the employer, the plan is considered unfunded. In a fully funded pension plan, the entire amount that has been recognized as an expense has been transferred to the trustee; in a partially funded plan, the funds that are transferred cover only part of the recognized expense. Almost all large pension plans in the United States are either fully or partially funded.

The Employee Retirement Income Security Act (ERISA) of 1974 established statutory rules providing for a minimum contribution level and establishing participation and vesting policies. For many years, tax rules have provided a maximum deductible amount that effectively restricts companies' contributions. The amount recognized as pension expense in the financial statements does not necessarily correspond to the amount contributed to the plan.

Pension expense is determined by GAAP, which requires the cost of the employee's pension benefits to be recognized in accordance with the accrual accounting objective, under which revenues are recognized when earned and expenses are recognized when incurred rather than when cash is received or paid. As a result, account-ants treat the funding of pensions and the recognition of pension expense as two distinct events.

One simple test of a company's ability to meet its future pension benefit obligations is to compare pension fund assets to vested benefit liabilities. If the balance in pension fund assets is smaller than that in vested benefit liabilities, the company may face liquidity problems in the future, particularly if its economic prospects decline. The information needed to make this analysis is in the footnotes to the financial statements.

24

TREASURY STOCK

Treasury stock is a corporation's own stock that has been issued and subsequently reacquired by the corporation and often reissued at a later date. Companies purchase their own stock for a variety of reasons:

1. To hold for employee stock purchase plans
2. To thwart a takeover by another company
3. To support the price of the common stock
4. To reduce shares outstanding and thereby increase earnings per share
5. To use in the acquisition of other companies

For whatever reason, the acquisition of treasury stock is commonplace; in 1989, Coca-Cola reported 81,894,886 common shares held as treasury stock. A corporation cannot own a part of itself, so treasury stock is never considered an asset. The acquisition of treasury stock means a reduction in stockholders' equity, because of the cash outlay. Further, the income statement is never affected by the purchase or sale of treasury stock. When treasury stock is acquired, it is generally recorded at its cost, and when it is sold or issued, any difference between its costs and the cash received is recorded in the Additional Paid-in Capital account.

For example, assume a firm's stockholders' equity section appears as follows:

STOCKHOLDERS' EQUITY

Common stock, 10,000 shares issued and outstanding	$150,000
Additional paid-in capital	80,000
Retained earnings	550,000
Total stockholders' equity	$780,000

Assume the corporation buys back 1,000 of its own shares at a price of $15 per share. Its stockholders' equity section then appears:

STOCKHOLDERS' EQUITY

Common stock, 10,000 shares and 9,000 outstanding	$150,000
Additional paid-in capital	80,000
Retained earnings	550,000
	$780,000
Deduct Treasury stock (1000 shares) at cost	15,000
Total stockholders' equity	$765,000

Note that the common stock and additional paid-in capital account balances are not affected by the transaction. However, the cost of the shares is deducted from stockholders' equity. In addition, the number of treasury shares is disclosed, so that the total number of shares issued and outstanding can be determined. In this case, the number of shares issued is 10,000, and the number of shares in the treasury is 1,000. The difference of 9,000 shares is the number of shares outstanding (stock owned by the existing stockholders).

If treasury stock is reissued, any difference between its cost and the cash received is recorded in the Additional Paid-in Capital account. To illustrate, assume that 500 shares of treasury stock are reissued and sold for $18 a share. The difference between the cost of the treasury stock ($15) and the amount received ($18) increases additional paid-in capital. The stockholders' equity section then appear as follows:

STOCKHOLDERS' EQUITY

Common stock, 10,000 shares issued and 9,500 outstanding	$150,000
Additional paid-in capital	81,500
Retained earnings	550,000
	$781,500
Deduct Treasury stock (500 shares) at cost	7,500
	$775,000

25

REVENUE RECOGNITION

Revenues represent the amount received when a business sells a product or provides services to a customer. Revenues are typically measured by the amount of cash received or expected to be received from the transaction. Two conditions must be met before revenues can be recorded: (1) the amount of revenue must be able to be measured objectively, and (2) the company must have completed or substantially completed the activities it must perform to be entitled to the revenues.

Both of these criteria are generally considered to be satisfied at the point of sale—when the product is delivered to the customer or when the service is provided. At this point, the seller has fulfilled or substantially fulfilled his or her obligation and the revenue is measured by the exchange price between the buyer and seller.

Although revenue is generally recognized at the point of sale, certain exceptions to this rule exist. One exception is used in the percentage-of-completion method, accounting for long-term projects. Many companies engage in long-term construction projects of several years' duration, such as building ships, commercial aircraft, and weapons delivery systems. In these instances, it is appropriate to recognize revenue over a project's life rather than wait until it is completed. Under the percentage-of-completion method, revenues and profit are allocated to each period based upon the progress toward completion, which is usually computed by comparing the current period's construction cost to the total cost expected for the project.

For example, assume that Bridgebuilder, Inc., signed a $12 million contract to build a bridge over three years. Bridgebuilder's accounting department estimates total construction costs of $10 million, with a projected profit of $2 million. The following schedule shows the revenues and profit that should be recognized each year:

Year	(1) Actual Costs Incurred	(2) Percentage of Work Completed	(3) Revenue Recognized	(4) Profit Recognized
1	$3,000,000	30%	$3,600,000	$600,000
2	6,000,000	60%	7,200,000	1,200,000
3	1,200,000	Remainder	1,800,000 (Remainder)	0 (Remainder)

For the first two years, the percentage of work completed is determined by dividing the actual costs incurred by the $10 million construction costs. The resulting percentage is then multiplied by the contract price of $12 million to get revenue for the year and by the estimated profit of $2 million to get the profit recognized for that year. In year 3, the last year of the contract, we are no longer estimating the total cost of the project and the profit earned. Since total construction costs turned out to be $10.2 million instead of $10 million, the overall profit on the project is $1.8 million instead of the projected $2 million. Since the amount of revenue recognized in the first two years totaled $10.8 million ($3.6 million + $7.2 million) and the amount of profit totaled ($1.8 million), revenue and profit recognized in the third year are $1.8 million ($12 million − $10.8 million) and 0 ($1.8 million − $1.8 million), respectively.

26

DEPRECIATION

In everyday language, depreciation means the decline in the market value of an asset. For example, an automobile that initially costs $15,000 is said to depreciate by $3,000 if its resale value at the end of the year is $12,000. In this context, depreciation refers to the decline in the market value of the asset.

From a financial accounting standpoint, however, depreciation is not a measure of the change in the market value of the asset but rather a systematic method of allocating the original cost of the asset to expense over the asset's useful life. To illustrate, assume a machine costs $100,000 and has an anticipated life of ten years and no estimated salvage value at the end of the ten years. Each year over the asset's life we recognize a portion of the $100,000 cost as depreciation expense until, by the end of the tenth year, the entire $100,000 cost of the asset has been written off (recognized as expense). On the balance sheet, the total depreciation taken on the asset (the total amount of depreciation expense deducted on the income statement) is accumulated in an account called accumulated depreciation. Accumulated depreciation is deducted from the cost of the asset on the balance sheet to yield the book value of the asset. An example of this presentation is as follows:

Machinery	$300,000
Less Accumulated Depreciation	75,000
	$225,000

Several alternative methods of calculating depreciation are available. In each method, the amount to be depreciated (asset's cost minus its expected salvage value) is spread over the asset's useful life, and the total depreciation expense to be recognized remains the same. However, the different methods of depreciation yield different amounts of depreciation expense to be recognized in a given year.

The methods of depreciation can be divided into two broad categories: straight-line depreciation and accelerated depreciation. Under straight-line depreciation, the same amount of depreciation is recognized each year. Accelerated depreciation methods result in greater depreciation expense and lower net income during the early years of the asset's life than does straight-line depreciation, and lower depreciation expense and higher net income during the later years of the asset's life.

Most businesses use straight-line depreciation in preparing the financial statements to be distributed to external users because it results in lower depreciation expense in the early years of an asset's life and thus higher reported earnings. In later years, when accelerated depreciation is lower than straight-line depreciation, total depreciation expense using the straight-line method may still be less than under an accelerated method if the amount invested in new assets continues to grow.

When reporting to the Internal Revenue Service, most companies use accelerated depreciation because the higher depreciation expense results in lower taxable income and taxes in the earlier years of an asset's life, and the business can use the money that would have been paid in taxes to generate additional income.

Companies may choose one method of depreciation for financial reporting and a different one for tax purposes. In fact, companies usually do choose different methods, because the accelerated methods are more attractive for tax purposes than for accounting purposes.

In 1981, the Internal Revenue Code was amended to permit the use of the Accelerated Cost Recovery System (ACRS), which follows a depreciation pattern very similar to that of accelerated depreciation, for depreciable assets put into service after 1980.

The principal depreciation calculation methods used for financial reporting are:
1. Straight-line depreciation
2. Units of production
3. Sum-of-the-years' digits
4. Double-declining-balance

Each of these methods is illustrated in the following example.

Example:

Cost	$100,000
Estimated salvage value	$10,000
Estimated life in years	5
Estimated life in units of output	20,000
Output this year	5,000

a. Straight-line depreciation:

$$\frac{\text{Cost} - \text{Estimated salvage value}}{\text{Estimated useful life}}$$

$$= \frac{\$100,000 - \$10,000}{5 \text{ years}}$$

$$= \$18,000 \text{ per year}$$

b. Units of production depreciation:
Depreciation expense per unit =

$$\frac{\text{Cost} - \text{Estimated salvage value}}{\text{Estimated total units to be produced}}$$

$$= \frac{\$100,000 - 10,000}{20,000 \text{ units}}$$

$$= \$4.50 \text{ per unit}$$

Depreciation expense each year = Depreciation expense per unit multiplied by the number of units produced that year:

$$= \$4.50 \times 5,000 \text{ units}$$
$$= \$22,500$$

c. Sum-of-the-years'-digits depreciation:
   Cost − estimated salvage value ×

   $$\frac{\text{Remaining life}}{\text{Sum of digits of years of life}}$$

   $$= (\$100,000 - \$10,000) \times \frac{5 \text{ years}}{1 + 2 + 3 + 4 + 5}$$

   $$= \$90,000 \times \frac{5 \text{ years}}{15 \text{ years}}$$

   $$= \$30,000$$

   $$\text{Year 2} = (\$100,000 - 10,000) \times \frac{4 \text{ years}}{1 + 2 + 3 + 4 + 5}$$

   $$= \$90,000 \times \frac{4 \text{ years}}{15 \text{ years}}$$

   $$= 24,000$$

d. Double-declining-balance depreciation:
   Double the straight-line depreciation rate × asset's book value (cost − accumulated depreciation) at the beginning of the year.

The straight-line depreciation rate $= \dfrac{1}{\text{life in years}}$

$$= \dfrac{1}{5}$$

$$= 20\%$$

Double the straight-line depreciation rate is 40%

Yr 1 = \$100,000 × 40% = \$40,000
Yr 2 = (\$100,000 − \$40,000) × 40% = \$24,000
Yr 3 = (\$100,000 − \$40,000 − \$24,000) × 40%
      = \$9,600

The sum-of-the-years'-digits depreciation method and the double-declining-balance depreciation method are both examples of accelerated methods, with depreciation highest early in the life of the asset and declining thereafter.

27

DEPLETION

Depletion is the using up of natural resources such as coal, timber, minerals, and crude oil. These assets are sometimes called "wasting" assets, because they are actually consumed, in contrast to assets such as equipment, which can be reused.

The accounting for depletion closely parallels the accounting for the depreciation of property, plant, and equipment. Depletion and depreciation are similar except that they apply to different assets. Natural resources are initially recorded at cost, which includes the cash necessary to acquire the resources, legal fees, surveying costs, and exploration costs. Subsequently, the extraction or consumption of the resources is recognized as depletion expense using a computation essentially indentical to the units-of-production depreciation method.

Depletion expense is calculated using a two-step process. First, the cost of the natural resources less any salvage value is divided by the number of units estimated to be in the resource deposit to obtain depletion expense per unit. This figure is then multiplied by the number of units extracted during a given period to compute the depletion expense to be deducted on that period's income statement.

For example, assume $10 million was invested in a coal mine estimated to have 40 million tons of coal. In the first year, 5 million tons were extracted and sold. The first step involves the computation of depletion expense per ton:

$$\$10,000 \div 40,000,000 \text{ tons} = \$.25 \text{ per ton}$$

The next step is to multiply the depletion expense per ton times the tons extracted and sold that period:

$.25 × $5,000,000 = $1,250,000 depletion expense

Depletion expense of $1,250,000 is then deducted in the income statement, and the balance sheet total for the coal mine is reduced from $10,000,000 to $8,750,000 ($10,000,000 − $1,250,000).

28

UNUSUAL INCOME STATEMENT ITEMS

Users of financial statements are extremely interested in the periodic earnings reported by a company. Current income influences the amount of dividends to be distributed as well as the market price of the stock. In addition, current income is a starting point for predicting future income. For these reasons, the income statement should be presented in a way that enhances its usefulness to investors, creditors, and users of financial statements.

To achieve this goal, the accounting profession requires that business income from the recurring activities of the company be segregated from income produced by unusual and uncommon transactions and events, making it easier for users to evaluate the performance of the company and to predict future income. In predicting future income, it is the performance of recurring activities of the company that is important, not the results of transactions and events that are not expected to recur in the future. Two of the more frequently encountered unusual items are discontinued operations and extraordinary items.

Discontinued Operations. The term "discontinued operations" refers to operations of a segment of a business that has been sold, abandoned, spun off, or otherwise disposed of. A segment is a component whose activities represent a separate major line of business or class of customer; it may be a subsidiary, a division, or a department, as long as its activities can be clearly distinguished from other activities, both physically and operationally, for financial reporting purposes.

The income or loss of the discontinued operation is reported separately and appears on the income statement after a subtotal amount called income from continuing operations. Income from continuing operations is the income after taxes of the recurring operations of the business. The effect of this requirement is to separate the revenues, expenses, gains, and losses of discontinued operations from those of continuing operations.

The gain or loss from discontinued operations is computed by adding the segment's net income or loss for the period and the gain or loss on disposal of the segment. For example, if corporation ABC has four divisions and sells one, a condensed income statement would appear as follows:

Income from continuing operations		$1,110,000
Discontinued operation:		
Income from discontinued operations	$105,000	
Gain on disposal of the division	500,000	605,000
Net Income		$1,715,000

Extraordinary Items. Extraordinary items are material gains and losses that result from unusual events or transactions. These transactions are reported separately from the effects of continued operations and appear directly below discontinued operations on the income statement. They are separated from continued operations because by definition they are not expected to recur in the future.

To be classified as an extraordinary item, a transaction or event must be both unusual in nature and infrequent in occurrence. Notice that both criteria must be satisfied. A transaction or event is considered unusual if it possesses a high degree of abnormality and is unrelated to the ordinary and typical activities of the business. In deciding if an event is in fact extraordinary, one must consider the environment in which the company operates, taking into account factors such as industry characteristics, geographical location of facilities, and the extent of government regulation. Thus, earthquake damage in New York might qualify as extraordinary, whereas such damage in California might not.

The second criterion that must be met concerns frequency of occurrence. If an event or transaction occurs every five or ten years, it does not qualify as infrequent.

A good example of an extraordinary loss is a $36 million loss recognized by Weyerhaeuser Company as a result of volcanic activity at Mount St. Helens. Lava spewing from the volcano covered 68,000 acres owned by Weyerhaeuser and destroyed valuable timber.

29

CHANGE IN ACCOUNTING PRINCIPLE

To enhance the comparability of their financial statements, companies are expected to follow the same accounting methods or principles from one period to the next. Otherwise, it is impossible to evaluate the progress of the business by examining its financial statements.

Although the accounting profession advocates consistency, a company may change accounting methods if management can justify the change. If new methods are adopted, the effects must be clearly disclosed in the income statement. Examples of a change include a switch in depreciation methods (e.g., from double-declining balance to straight-line depreciation) and a change in inventory costing (e.g., from weighted-average to FIFO).

When a company changes its accounting methods and practices, it must compute the difference in the total net income reported in prior years and the income that would have been reported over the same period under the new principle. For example, assume that Amato Corporation has decided to switch from recording depreciation by the double-declining balance method to using straight-line depreciation. If the latter had been used in previous years, net income would have been $75,000 greater. This increase must be reported at the bottom of the income statement and described as follows: Cumulative effect on prior years of a change in depreciation method—$75,000.

30

EARNINGS PER SHARE

Earnings per share (EPS)—the net income or earnings per share of common stock—is probably the most publicized and relied-upon financial statistic. Because of its importance, investors should know how EPS is computed as well as its usefulness and its limitations.

EPS has been called a summary indicator, because in one single item it communicates substantial information about a company's performance. Many financial statement users focus upon summary indicators as a way to bypass complete financial statements, which can be difficult to understand. However, overreliance on EPS can have severe pitfalls. Misleading inferences can be drawn if the calculations that yield EPS on the income statement are ignored. Details in the income statement, such as trends in gross profit, may be more important than EPS. Further, an analysis of the firm's total operations and financial condition requires more information that can be garnered simply by examining EPS.

In its most basic form, EPS is calculated by dividing total earnings by the number of shares outstanding. (Accountants use the term "earnings" interchangeably with "net income" and "net profit.") When preferred stock has been issued, net income is reduced by the dividends payable to preferred stockholders:

$$\frac{\text{Net Income} - \text{Preferred Dividends}}{\text{Average Common Shares Outstanding}} = \text{EPS}$$

However, this presentation is inadequate when companies have issued convertible securities, stock options, warrants, or other financial instruments that can be exchanged for or converted to common shares at some future time. The presence of these securities means that the number of common shares outstanding may increase in the future, resulting in a dilution (reduction) of EPS.

To illustrate, assume a firm has common stock outstanding of 1 million shares and 100,000 shares of convertible preferred stock, each share of which can be converted into one share of common stock. If net income is $50,000 and dividends of $20,000 are payable to preferred shareholders, EPS may be calculated as follows:

$$\text{EPS} = \frac{\$500,000 - \$20,000}{1,000,000 \text{ shares}} = \$.48$$

If the convertible preferred stock is converted into common stock, EPS will be diluted. Assuming conversion at the beginning of the year:

$$\text{EPS} = \frac{\$500,000 - 0}{1,100,000 \text{ shares}} = \$.45$$

The potential earnings dilution is thus $.03 per share.

If a business has issued securities that would significantly dilute EPS if they were to be converted into common stock, a dual presentation of EPS is required. Accountants refer to these EPS figures as "primary earnings per share" and fully diluted earnings per share." Although the complex rules are beyond the scope of this book, primary earnings per share assume that certain dilutive securities are converted into common stock. Fully diluted earnings per share, however, is based upon the assumption that all dilutive securities were converted into common shares at the beginning of the period. Fully diluted EPS must always be less than or equal to primary EPS. Note that the calculation of fully diluted EPS assumes that conversion of all contingent issuances will occur, which may never be the case.

Earnings per share are disclosed in the following manner:

PRESENTATION OF EARNINGS PER SHARE
(Bottom of the income statement)

Net income	$400,000
Earnings per share:	
Primary earnings per share	$2.85
Fully diluted earnings per share	$2.70

31

CONSOLIDATED FINANCIAL STATEMENTS

A company that owns more than 50 percent of the common stock of another company is known as the parent company, and the company whose stock is owned by the parent company is called the subsidiary company. One parent may have several subsidiaries; in fact, some companies known as conglomerates have many.

It is not necessary for the majority stockholder to own 100 percent of the stock for the parent/subsidiary relationship to exist or for the parent to exercise sufficient control to maintain that relationship. The other stockholders, in a non-wholly owned subsidiary, are referred to as minority shareholders.

Generally, the financial statements issued by the parent company, called consolidated financial statements, include the assets, liabilities, revenues, and expenses of not only the parent company but its subsidiaries as well. Consolidated financial statements ignore the distinction between the parent and subsidiary organizations and present the income statement, balance sheet, and statement of cash flows of a single entity rather than separate financial statements for each entity.

Generally, consolidation involves combining the separate components' financial statements. However, some transactions between the parent and the subsidiary must be eliminated to prevent the assets, liabilities, revenues, and expenses of the parent and its subsidiaries being overstated in the consolidated financial statements. For example, assume Parent Company borrows $10,000 from Sub Company by signing a note payable. The transaction appears on the balance sheet of both companies as follows:

Parent Company Balance Sheet		Subsidiary Company Balance Sheet	
Assets		Assets	
Notes payable	$10,000	Notes receivable	$10,000

The consolidated financial statement is supposed to reflect transactions between the parent/subsidiary group and all outside entities. In this example, if the two balance sheets were simply added together, the consolidated balance sheet would indicate that the parent/subsidiary unit expects to both receive and pay $10,000 in the near future. This disclosure would be incorrect because the $10,000 represents a future transfer of cash from the parent to the subsidiary, both of which are part of the same economic unit; the parent/subsidiary unit does not have a claim on any outside party, nor does it owe any outsider. To reflect properly this transaction, neither the note receivable nor the note payable should appear on the companies' consolidated balance sheet.

32

SEGMENT REPORTING

Consolidated financial statements total the accounting results of the segments of diversified companies. However, presenting those results separately for each segment makes it easier to understand the financial position and prospects of a diversified company. Generally accepted accounting principles (GAAP) provide rules for reporting segment information, which is typically disclosed in the footnotes to the financial statements. The financial reports of companies with publicly traded securities provide four different types of segment information:

1. Results for different industries
2. Foreign operations and geographic areas
3. Export sales
4. Major customers

An industry segment is a unit of a company that provides a product or service, primarily to unaffiliated companies, at a profit. Reportable segments as defined by GAAP are determined by:

• Identifying the individual products and services that produce revenue.
• Grouping these products and services into industry segments.
• Selecting those segments that are significant in relation to the company as a whole.

Since no single set of characteristics can determine the industry segments of all companies, management judgment must play a significant role in the selection of segments. Three factors should be considered by management in determining segments:

1. The nature of the product.
2. The nature of the production process.
3. Markets and marketing methods.

After the segments are determined, the company decides which segments are sufficiently significant to be reportable. Under GAAP, an industry segment is regarded as significant and therefore reportable if one of the following tests is satisfied:

1. Its revenue is 10 percent or more of combined segment revenue.
2. Its operating profit or loss is 10 percent or more of the greater of combined profits of segments reporting profits or combined losses of segments reporting losses.
3. Its identifiable assets are 10 percent or more of combined segment identifiable assets.

Each reportable segment must disclose the following separately:

1. **Revenues**—sales of products to unaffiliated customers as well as sales to other segments.
2. **Operating profit or loss**—operating profit or loss reported for each segment.
3. **Identifiable assets**—including tangible and intangible assets.
4. **Other information**—other related disclosures, including (a) the aggregate amount of depreciation, depletion, and amortization expense for each segment, (b) the amount of each reportable segment's capital expenditures, and (c) types of products and services for each reportable segment.

Companies are also required to present segment information about foreign operations (those revenue-producing operations located outside the United States that generate revenues either from sales to unaffiliated customers or to other segments of the organization). Information must be disclosed for foreign operations if either (a) revenues received from sales of the foreign operations to unaffiliated customers are at least 10 percent of total organizational revenues, or (b) identifiable assets of the foreign operations are at least 10 percent of total organizational assets. Similarly, information must be disclosed for any geographic area in which sales to unaffiliated customers account for 10 percent or more of total organizational revenues or in which identifiable assets are 10 percent or more of total organizational assets. The required disclosures for foreign operations and geographical areas include sales to unaffiliated customers, inter-area sales, operating profit or loss, and identifiable assets.

An organization must disclose information about the extent of its reliance on its major customers, and users of financial statements should be aware of the threat to the company's continued profitability if one or several customers is lost. If 10 percent or more of the revenue of a company is derived from sale to a single customer, defined as either a group of entities under common control or a federal, state, or local government, the company must disclose this fact, as well as the amount of revenues from each such customer and the identity of the selling segment.

33

QUARTERLY FINANCIAL STATEMENTS

Companies listed by the Securities and Exchange Commission or whose stock is traded on the New York and American Stock Exchanges are required to prepare quarterly financial statements. The accounting profession considers each quarterly period to be an integral part of an annual period; and, with certain exceptions, the Generally Accepted Accounting Principles used by companies in the preparation of their latest annual financial statements also apply to quarterly reports. Quarterly financial statements are required for the first three quarters of the annual period; no fourth quarter report is required, because the annual financial statements include the results for all four periods.

Estimated figures that would not be acceptable in the annual report are acceptable in quarterly statements. For example, business may estimate the ending inventory for the quarter, rather than taking an actual inventory count, and may use their best estimate of the effective tax rate expected to be applicable for the full fiscal year in providing for income taxes. The tax estimate should be based on annual income from continuing operations.

At a minimum, publicly traded corporations presenting quarterly financial statements should disclose:

1. Sales or gross revenues, provisions for income taxes, extraordinary items, cumulative effect of a change in accounting principles or practices, and net income

2. Primary and fully diluted EPS
3. Seasonal revenues, costs, and expenses
4. Significant changes in estimates or provisions for income taxes
5. Disposals of business segments
6. Extraordinary, unusual, or infrequently occurring items
7. Contingent items
8. Changes in accounting principles or estimates
9. Significant changes in financial position

34

NOTES TO FINANCIAL STATEMENTS

In addition to the information contained in the body of the basic financial statements, accounting reports contain footnote (or note) disclosures that are essentially an extension of the basic financial statements. Footnotes can usually be classified as follows:

• **Explanations of management's choices.** The footnotes describe the specific choices made by management in cases in which alternative accounting methods are acceptable. Examples include the selection of a depreciation method and an inventory valuation method.

• **A detailed description of broad captions in the financial statements.** Examples include a detailed breakdown on the pension obligation, the composition of property, plant, and equipment, and maturity dates for long-term debt.

• **Supplemental information.** Examples include significant events or transactions that occur subsequent to the balance sheet date but prior to the issuance of the financial statements.

The order in which footnotes are presented varies greatly, but they should follow a logical sequence. The footnotes often appear in the order in which they are referred to in the financial statements.

The first footnote is usually a description of the accounting policies followed by the business. In addition to explaining management's choice of accounting

method, footnote disclosure also is used to discuss policies in these areas:
- Consolidation
- Net income per common share
- Inventories
- Property, plant, and equipment
- Intangible assets
- Income taxes
- Pensions
- Stock options and stock purchsae plans
- Long-term contracts
- Marketable securities
- Foreign currency

35

AUDITOR'S OPINION

Financial statements are a key aspect of the annual report issued by a corporation to its shareholders, and an examination of the statements should include a reading of the auditor's opinion. An auditor is an independent third party, usually a representative of a public accounting firm or an individual CPA, who conducts an examination of the accounting information presented in the annual report.

The results of the examination are reflected in the independent auditor's report, which usually has three relatively brief paragraphs emphasizing that:

1. The financial statements are the responsibility of management.
2. The financial statements have been audited in a manner that provides reasonable assurance that they are free of material misstatement.
3. The statements, in the auditor's opinion, are or are not fairly presented and in all material respects in conformity with generally accepted accounting principles (GAAP).

The auditor usually issues a standard unqualified or "clean" opinion indicating that, in all material aspects, the financial statements present fairly the financial position, the results of operations, and the changes in cash flows in conformity with GAAP applied on a consistent basis. An unqualified opinion does not imply that the auditor has made a favorable judgment about the business's current financial condition or its future prospects, only that its financial disclosures accurately reflect the company's financial position. The purpose of an audit is to foster confidence in management's disclosures; it is intended to provide assurance that the financial statements are a fair representation of a company's economic activities and events.

An unqualified opinion appears as follows:

Independent Auditor's Report

We have audited the accompanying balance sheets of X company as of December 31, 19X2 and 19X1 and the related statements of income, retained earnings, and cash flows for the years then ended. These financial statements are the responsibility of the company's management. Our responsibility is to express an opinion on these financial statements based on our audits.

We conducted our audits in accordance with generally accepted auditing standards. Those standards require that we plan and perform the audit to obtain reasonable assurance about whether the financial statements are free of material misstatement. An audit includes examining, on a test basis, evidence supporting the amounts and disclosures in the financial statements. An audit also includes assessing the accounting principles used and significant estimates made by management, as well as evaluating the overall financial statement presentation. We believe that our audits provide a reasonable basis for our opinion.

In our opinion, the financial statements referred to above present fairly, in all material respects, the financial position of X Company as of December 31, 19X2 and 19X1, and the results of its operations and its cash flows for the years then ended in conformity with generally accepted accounting principles.

Date   Auditor's signature

Although most audit reports receive an unqualified opinion, some reports do express reservations about the fairness of the statements. An auditor can issue a qualified opinion, for example, if an accounting procedure represents a departure from GAAP or if the auditor's appraisal of the financial statements has been hindered by incomplete or poorly kept client records. A qualified audit report typically includes the phrase "except for," followed by the nature of the qualification.

36

FINANCIAL LEVERAGE

Financial leverage is the use of debt to magnify returns. Speculators attempt to multiply returns by supplementing their own funds with borrowed funds, and businesses use financial leverage to increase net income and increase the resources available to generate future profits. Leveraging is successful as long as the money borrowed produces returns greater than the interest charges incurred on the debt. However, debt involves risk because the business commits itself to making fixed interest payments; if it defaults, it becomes insolvent. Financial leverage is illustrated in the following example.

Assume ABC Corporation has $1 million in total assets and that the company's capital structure (liabilities plus owners' or stockholders' equity) consists of 60 percent debt and 40 percent equity:

Assets	$2,000,000
Liabilities	$1,200,000
Owners' equity	$ 800,000

Assume the cost of debt is 10 percent and the company has an average tax rate of 30 percent. If ABC Corporation has operating income of $400,000, the return on owners' equity is

Operating income	$400,000
Interest expense	120,000
Income before tax	280,000
Income tax expense	84,000
Net income	$196,000

$$\frac{\text{Net income}}{\text{Owners' equity}} = \frac{196,000}{800,000} = 24.5\%$$

If ABC Corporation increases net income by 20 percent to $480,000, the return on owners' equity increases from 24.5 percent to 31.5 percent, an increase slightly in excess of 28 percent.

Operating income	$480,000
Interest expense	120,000
Income before tax	360,000
Income tax expense	108,000
Net income	$252,000

$$\frac{\text{Net income}}{\text{Owners' equity}} = \frac{\$252,000}{\$800,000} = 31.5\%$$

In other words, a 20 percent increase in income produces a 28 percent increase in owners' equity. In this case, leverage works for the owners. Interest is a fixed charge; the income generated by using debt in excess of the interest charges accrues to the benefit of stockholders.

Conversely, leverage can harm the owners of a business. ABC Corporation's operating income drops by 20 percent to $320,000, the return on equity will drop from 24.5 percent to 17.5 percent, a decrease of slightly more than 28 percent:

Operating income	$320,000
Interest expense	120,000
Income before tax	200,000
Income tax expense	60,000
Net income	$140,000

$$\frac{\text{Net income}}{\text{Owners' equity}} = \frac{\$140,000}{\$800,000} = 17.5\%$$

In this case, a 20 percent drop in operating income reduces the return on owners' equity by 28%. Highly leveraged companies can suffer steep declines in income when a downturn in the economy occurs.

37

FUNDAMENTAL ANALYSIS

Financial statements are essential in fundamental analysis; a method for predicting future stock prices by estimating a security's value (its *intrinsic value*) based on financial and economic facts about the issuing company and comparing it to the current market price. If the current market price is less than the intrinsic value, a buy recommendation is issued; alternatively, if the current market price is greater than the intrinsic value, a sell recommendation is called for.

(An alternative method of security analysis, called technical analysis, studies historical trends in stock price movements and other market variables in order to predict future stock prices. Technical analysts use indicators, charts, and computer programs to track prices and predict future trends and often reject the analysis of financial and economic variables as too burdensome and time-consuming to be useful in evaluating security prices.)

Intrinsic value—the price at which a security should sell under normal conditions—is determined by evaluating such factors as net assets (assets minus liabilities), earnings, dividends, prospects (or risk), of future earnings and dividends, and management capability. Also critical to fundamental analysis is the evaluation of earnings, particularly future earnings. Most fundamental analysts cite the expectation of future earnings as the single most important variable affecting security prices.

The analysis of earnings is not a simple task. Fundamental analysts cannot use reported earnings alone as a guide to future earnings. Earnings are affected by accounting decisions such as how to determine depreciation expense and cost of goods sold (both of which can be recorded using any one of several alternatives). In addition, the computation of net income ignores increments in the market value of assets and fails to take into account the omission of certain assets and liabilities, such as brand names and obligations for future health benefits of employees, from the financial statements.

Fundamental analysts must estimate "true" or "economic" earnings, a measure that reflects the change in the wealth of an entity. Economic earnings frequently differ by more than 20 percent from the earnings reported by accountants, and should, if developed properly, be a better measure of the capacity of the firm to pay future dividends and generate future earnings.

The evaluation of earnings typically involves the appraisal of four earnings factors:

1. Level of economic earnings as well as reported earnings
2. Current and future dividends
3. Expectations of future earnings
4. Predictability of future earnings and dividends

Predictable earnings are more highly valued by analysts than earnings which cannot be forecast. Similarly, earnings that follow a steady upward path are more highly valued than volatile earnings with a higher trend.

Intrinsic value changes as factors that affect stock prices (e.g., earnings and dividends) change, and stock prices change with the economic prospects of the company. However, stock prices fluctuate around the intrinsic value if it is accurately estimated. External factors such as pessimism or optimism may cause temporary gaps between the intrinsic value and the market price of a security; fundamental analysts believe they can exploit these gaps by buying common stock when it sells at a price less than intrinsic value and selling common stock when its price exceeds intrinsic value.

38

RED FLAGS

Many investors and creditors are discouraged from using financial statements and the related footnotes because of their complexity. And, indeed, a thorough knowledge of financial statements of a company of any size can require considerable time and effort. But it is possible to glean important information about a company's prospects by spending several minutes looking for specific indications of potential problems.

Clues that a company may be heading for trouble include:

• **Earnings problems.** One of the most significant red flags is a downward trend in earnings. Companies are required to disclose earnings for the last three years in the income statement, so don't look just at the "bottom line." The trend in operating income is just as important as the trend in earnings.

• **Reduced cash flow.** To a certain extent, management can exploit GAAP to produce the appearance of increased earnings. Some popular shenanigans include booking sales on long-term contracts before the customer has paid up, delaying the recording of expenses, failing to recognize the obsolescence of inventory as an expense, and reducing advertising and research and development expenditures. You can use the cash flow statement to check the reliability of earnings. If net income is moving up while cash flow from operations is drifting downward, something may be wrong.

• **Excessive debt.** Crucial to determining whether a company can weather difficult times is the debt factor. Companies burdened by too much debt lack the financial flexibility to respond to crises and to take advantage of opportunities. Small companies with heavy debt are particularly vulnerable in economic downturns. Investment professionals pay special attention to a company's debt-to-equity ratio, the proportion of total debt to stockholders' or owners' equity. While the optimum ratio varies from industry to industry, the amount of stockholders' or owners' equity should *significantly* exceed the amount of debt by a significant amount. This information is available on the balance sheet.

• **Overstated inventories and receivables.** Look at the ratio of accounts receivable to sales and the ratio of inventory to cost of goods sold. If accounts receivable exceeds 15 percent of annual sales and inventory exceeds 25 percent of cost of goods sold, be careful. If customers aren't paying their bills and/or the company is saddled with aging merchandise, problems will eventually arise. Overstated inventories and receivables are often at the heart of corporate fraud. As significant as the ratios are trends over time. Although there may be good reasons for a company to have high or increasing inventory or receivables, it's important to determine if the condition is a symptom of financial difficulty.

39

LIMITATIONS OF BUSINESS FINANCIAL STATEMENTS

Although financial statements provide useful information, they have definite limitations. For example, accountants do not include as assets certain items that are critical to the growth and well-being of a company. The quality of its employees is probably the most significant asset for many businesses, yet this vital asset is nowhere reflected in the balance sheet. Although this omission is understandable, it is a definite limitation.

The balance sheet seldom discloses the current market values of assets. Although historical cost is defended by accountants as an objective, reliable method of valuation, it is clearly less useful to the decisions of users than current market values of assets.

In addition, the estimates used to determine depreciation, collectibility of receivables, salability of inventory, pension expense, warranty costs, and other items that affect both the income statement and balance sheet, may not be accurate. Users frequently rely on accounting numbers without realizing how important estimates are in producing those numbers.

Finally, accounting numbers are affected by the choice of accounting methods made by the company. The choice of accounting method can have a significant impact on the income reported in the income statement and the value of the asset reported in the balance sheet.

40

PERSONAL FINANCIAL STATEMENTS: THE BALANCE SHEET

Financial statements should be used to assess the financial condition of an individual or a family. The two most useful financial statements for individuals or families are the balance sheet and the income statement; both statements are necessary for a thorough understanding of a person's financial condition.

The balance sheet describes an individual's or a family's financial condition at a particular time by providing a listing of assets, liabilities, and net worth. It's a good idea to review your financial assets and liabilities at least once a year, and to compare balance sheets over time to evaluate financial progress and to provide direction in planning for the future. Applications for personal loans and home mortgages ask for the information presented in a balance sheet.

A personal balance sheet is organized into three parts: assets, liabilities, and net worth. Assets—the items that you own—are listed at their current market value. Note that this is in contrast to business balance sheets, which list assets at their acquisition cost. Liabilities represent the dollar value of your debts, and net worth is the difference between your assets and liabilities.

Assets can be classified as either monetary, tangible, or investment. Monetary assets are cash or assets that are highly liquid. Tangible assets are physical assets with long lives. Although tangible assets can be sold to raise cash, they are primarily a means to maintaining a person's lifestyle. Investment assets are those purchased to generate income or in the hope that they will increase in value. Examples of the different kinds of assets include:

Monetary Assets
- Cash (including savings accounts, checking accounts, savings bonds, money market accounts)
- Money owed to you

Tangible Assets
- Automobile
- House, condominium, vacation home
- Furniture and appliances
- Personal property

Investment Assets
- Stocks, bonds, mutual funds
- Real estate investments
- Cash value of life insurance and annuities
- Company pension plans

Liabilities, the current market value of the debts you owe to others, are divided into short-term (payable within one year) and long-term. Examples of liabilities include:

Short-Term Liabilities
- Unpaid bills
- Taxes
- Insurance premiums
- Rent
- Utilities
- Charge accounts

Long-Term Liabilities
- Automobile loans
- Bank loans
- Education loans
- Home mortgage

Net worth is the difference between assets and liabilities. In equation form, it can be represented as:

$$\text{Assets} - \text{Liabilities} = \text{Net worth}$$

EXHIBIT 7
Personal Balance Sheet
December 31, 1991

Assets:

Monetary assets:		
Cash on hand	$ 125	
Savings account	7,500	
Checking account	2,000	
Total monetary assets		$9,625

Tangible assets:		
Home	$125,000	
Automobile	9,500	
Personal property	11,000	
Total tangible assets		$145,500

Investment assets:		
Savings bonds	$ 5,000	
Common stocks	13,500	
Mutual funds	8,500	
Total investment assets		27,000

Total assets:		$182,125

Liabilities:

Short-term liabilities:		
Insurance premium	$ 275	
Utilities	225	
Charge accounts	350	
Total short-term liabilities		$ 850

Long-term liabilities:		
Home mortgage	$85,000	
Bank loan	6,500	
Education Loans	7,500	
Auto Loan	8,250	
Total long-term liabilities		$107,250

Total liabilities		$108,100
Net Worth		74,025
Total liabilities and net worth		$182,125

41

PERSONAL FINANCIAL STATEMENTS: THE INCOME STATEMENT

The second basic personal financial statement, the income statement, is a flow statement—it reveals the income or revenues earned and the expense incurred over a specific period of time. If you want to know how much you spent on food or housing in the past year, this statement provides that information.

The income statement is divided into three sections: revenues or income, expenses (expenditures), and net income (gain or loss). If revenues exceed expenses, you have a net gain that you can use to make additional investments; if your expenditures exceed your revenues, your wealth has declined during the period covered.

Examples of items classified as revenues include the following:
• Wages and salaries
• Loan payments made to you
• Commissions
• Interest
• Dividends
• Social Security payments
• Pensions
• Gains from sale of property

Expenses include all expenditures made during the period. A useful way to categorize expenses is to break them down into fixed and variable expenses. Fixed expenses are required payments that do not vary from period to period, whereas variable expenses are those that fluctuate and over which you may have some control. The following are some examples of fixed and variable expenses:

Fixed Expenses
- Housing (rent, mortgage payments)
- Taxes
- Insurance premiums
- Automobile payments
- Pension contributions
- Personal loan payments

Variable Expenses
- Food
- Clothing
- Medical expenses
- Household furnishings
- Personal items
- Alcohol
- Cigarettes
- Gambling
- Entertainment
- Gifts
- Recreation
- Savings
- Investments
- Vacation

The bottom line on the income statement is your net gain or loss—the amount remaining after the expenditures are subtracted from your income. For example, if your total income is $40,000 and your expenditures total $35,000, your net gain that year is $5,000:

$$\text{Total income} - \text{Total Expenses} = \text{Net Gain}$$
$$\$40,000 - \$35,000 = \$5,000$$

The $5,000 represents money available to be saved or invested. On the other hand, if your income is $35,000 and you have spent $40,000, you have realized a loss of $5,000 for the year.

$$\text{Total Income} - \text{Total Expenses} = (\text{Net Loss})$$
$$\$35,000 - \$40,000 = (\$5,000)$$

You should be concerned about such a result, because it means that your wealth has decreased by $5,000. In this case, you need to take steps to live within your income by either increasing your earnings or reducing spending. Look at your variable expenses to see which ones can be cut or eliminated.

Exhibit 8 illustrates how an income statement should appear

EXHIBIT 8
Income Statement
For the Year Ending December 31, 1991

Income:

Husband's gross income	$40,000	
Wife's gross income	20,000	
Interest	2,000	
Dividends	500	
Capital gains (sale of stock)	1,000	
Total Income		$63,500

Expenses

Fixed expenses		
Home mortgage	$14,000	
Auto loans	7,200	
Auto insurance	800	
Life insurance	800	
Federal income taxes	15,000	
State income taxes	1,500	
Social Security tax	4,300	$43,600

Variable expenses		
Food	$ 7,500	
Utilities	2,500	
Gasoline and oil	1,000	
Auto repairs	500	
Clothing	1,600	
Medical expenses	600	
Contributions	2,300	
Church	600	
Vacation	1,100	
Health club	800	18,500
Total Expenses		62,100
Net Gain		$ 1,400

42

USING PERSONAL FINANCIAL STATEMENTS

Your personal financial statements—the balance sheet and the income statement—should provide the information you need to assess your current financial position and monitor your progress toward your goals. Preparing financial statements is a useful activity because it takes the guesswork out of the appraisal of your financial condition.

To simplify the preparation of your financial statements, you should obtain a ledger (a financial record book), which is available at office supply stores. A ledger should include separate sections for assets, liabilities, revenues, and expenditures. You should set up a separate account for each item in the four categories and record each transaction in the appropriate account. For example, if you purchase a sofa for $1,200, an entry should be made in the ledger recognizing the acquisition of a $1,200 asset and an expenditure of $1,200. When you prepare your financial statements, the sofa will be reflected on the balance sheet at its fair market value and on the income statement as a $1,200 expenditure. If you borrowed the money to purchase the sofa, the $1,200 would be shown as a liability on the balance sheet rather than as an expenditure in the income statement. An effective recordkeeping system enhances financial planning; keeping your records current makes it less likely that you will forget to record transactions and simplifies the preparation of financial statements.

Evaluating Progress. Ratio analysis can be used to evaluate personal financial statements as well as business financial statements. These ratios enable you to evaluate your financial condition as well as your current performance. The following financial ratios are useful in evaluating your financial health:

• **Liquidity Ratio.** This ratio is computed by dividing your monetary assets by your short-term liabilities.

$$\text{Liquidity ratio} = \frac{\text{Monetary assets}}{\text{Short-term liabilities}}$$

Monetary assets include cash on hand, savings accounts, checking accounts, money market mutual funds, and bank money market funds—in other words, cash and near-cash items readily convertible into cash. Short-term liabilities (debts payable within one year) include personal loans, credit card balances, insurance premiums, and other unpaid bills. For example, if your monetary assets total $7,000 and your short-term liabilities total $28,000, the liquidity ratio is computed by dividing $7,000 by $28,000, yielding 0.25, or 25 percent. Another way to look at this ratio is that your monetary assets cover about 25 percent of your existing short-term debts. Although there is no hard-and-fast rule on what constitutes a desirable liquidity ratio, you should be prepared for unexpected events that may curtail your revenues or increase your expenditures.

• **Debt-to-Equity (Net Worth) Ratio.** This ratio is computed by dividing your total liabilities by your net worth.

$$\text{Debt-to-equity ratio} = \frac{\text{Total liabilities}}{\text{Net worth}}$$

Banks use this ratio to evaluate your ability to meet your debts. For example, assume your total liabilities equal $75,000 and your net worth is $400,000. Computation of the ratio yields debt-to-equity of 18.75 percent ($75,000

/ $400,000). Your balance sheet shows that your debts are only 18.75 percent of your total net worth.

• **Debt service ratio.** This ratio measures your ability to meet your monthly debt payments and is computed by dividing your monthly loan payments by your before-tax income.

$$\text{Debt service ratio} = \frac{\text{Total monthly loan payments}}{\text{Monthly gross (before-tax) income}}$$

For example, if your monthly loan payments total $2,000 and your before-tax income is $5,000, you have a debt service ratio of 0.40 × 100, or 40 percent. This ratio indicates a high level of debt. Many financial planners believe that debt should not exceed 33 percent of monthly pretax income; debt above that level puts a family at great risk if a wage earner becomes unemployed.

• **Savings ratio.** This ratio, which is developed from the income statement, evaluates your level of current savings. It is computed by dividing your net gain in wealth by your after-tax income.

$$\text{Savings ratio} = \frac{\text{Net gain}}{\text{Income after taxes}}$$

If your net gain this year was $2,000 and your after-tax income was $30,000, you have a savings ratio of .067 or 6.7 percent ($2,000 / $30,000). This ratio is in line with the typical savings ratio of American families which is about 5 to 6 percent. If you are saving for an important goal, you might want to increase this ratio.

43

THE SECURITIES AND EXCHANGE COMMISSION

Prior to the 1930s, the federal government did little to regulate securities markets. But the collapse of international securities markets during the Depression fostered widespread criticism of how these markets had operated. In an effort to restore investor confidence, Congress established the Securities and Exchange Commission (SEC), the purpose of which is to administer federal laws that require full and fair disclosure of material facts related to securities offered to the public for sale and empower the SEC to initiate litigation in instances of fraud. The principle laws administered by the SEC are the Securities Act of 1933 and the Securities Exchange Act of 1934.

The Securities Act of 1933 provides for the regulation of the initial public distribution of a corporation's securities and for full and fair disclosure of relevant information concerning such issues to prospective purchasers. Various civil and criminal penalties are assessed against those who misrepresent information required to be disclosed under this act. In addition, new issues sold publicly through the mails or in interstate commerce must be registered with the SEC on special forms that require information such as:

1. Description of the registrant's properties and business.
2. Description of significant provisions of the security

to be offered for sale and its relationship to the registrant's other capital securities.
3. Information about the management of the registrant.
4. Financial statements certified by independent public accounts.

A portion of the information contained in the registration statement is included in the company prospectus, which is prepared for public distribution and for the use of potential investors. The prospectus includes audited financial statements, information about the firm's history, a list of its large stockholders, and other relevant facts.

The Securities Exchange Act of 1934 provides protection to investors by regulating the trading of securities of publicly held companies in the secondary market (exchanges and over-the-counter markets in which securities are bought and sold subsequent to original issuance). Extensive reporting is required, along with continuous disclosure of company activities through annual, quarterly, and special reports. Form 10-K the annual report, must be filed with the SEC within 90 days after the end of the firm's fiscal year. It calls for a myriad of financial data, including financial statements, in addition to nonfinancial information such as the names of the corporate officers and directors and the extent of their ownership. Form 10-Q is the quarterly report of operations, it must be filed within 45 days of the close of each of the first three quarters and contains abbreviated financial and nonfinancial information. Form 8-K, a report of material events or corporate changes deemed of importance to company shareholders or to the SEC, must be filed within 15 days of the occurrence of the event. These forms are available to shareholders or prospective investors on request. Fraudulent representations made in the various filings required by this act can result in harsh penalties.

Federal statutes give the SEC the power to dictate the accounting principles to be followed in these reports, but as a matter of policy the SEC generally supports the private-sector rulemaking organization, the Financial Accounting Standards Board (FASB), discussed in Key 44. However, for registration statements and 10-K reports, the SEC requires accounting disclosures that are generally more extensive than those specified by generally accepted accounting principles.

44

FINANCIAL ACCOUNTING STANDARDS BOARD

The primary rulemaking body for the accounting profession since 1973 has been the Financial Accounting Standards Board (FASB), a private-sector organization responsible for establishing and improving generally accepted accounting principles (GAAP), a set of standards and procedures that serves as a general guide in the preparation of financial statements. (The term "generally accepted" means either that a rule has been formulated governing reporting in a given area or that over time a given practice has been accepted as appropriate because of its universal application.) GAAP, which have been developed to reflect experience, reasonable custom, and usage, are updated as economic conditions change. They must be observed in the preparation of financial statements for external users (e.g., creditors and investors).

Although the FASB is not a governmental agency, its authority depends primarily upon endorsement of its pronouncements by the Securities and Exchange Commission (SEC) (see Key 43). Under securities acts passed in 1933 and 1934, the SEC was given authority to establish accounting principles for those corporations that must comply with its reporting requirements (typically, those with at least $5 million in assets and/or 500 stockholders). Instead of itself mandating standards of practice for accountants, the SEC allows the FASB to establish and improve accounting standards subject to its oversight.

The FASB adheres to a lengthy due-process system in

setting new standards of practice. The FASB attempts to be responsive to the needs and viewpoints of the entire economic community (not just the accounting profession) and operates in full view of the public; consequently, the development of a new accounting standard can be a lengthy process.

Several factors influence the FASB's decisionmaking process:

1. The FASB consists of only seven members. More members would make the decisionmaking process unwieldy.

2. All FASB members are fully remunerated and serve full-time. Members must sever all connection with previous employers, reducing the possibility of conflicts of interest and ensuring greater independence. Currently, FASB members earn an annual salary of approximately $300,000. They are supported in their work by a staff of about forty professionals.

3. FASB members are selected from a variety of backgrounds so that the entire economic community, not only the accounting profession, is represented. On the current board three members have a public accounting background, two are former corporate officers, one is a former academic, and one is a past chief accountant of the SEC.

4. An affirmative vote of five of the seven FASB members is needed to approve a pronouncement.

The most important pronouncements of the FASB are the Statements of Financial Accounting Standards (SFAS), which establish new GAAP or amendments thereto. Since its inception, the FASB has issued over 100 SFAS's, some of them controversial.

One SFAS currently under consideration would require that health benefits for retirees be treated as a form of deferred compensation, similar to pensions, beginning in 1993. One study suggests that many companies' health costs will jump by three to six times if this ruling goes into effect.

QUESTIONS AND ANSWERS

What does a balance sheet disclose?

The balance sheet is like a snapshot that provides a picture of the financial health of a business at a particular point in time. Essentially, a balance sheet reveals what a business has, what it owes, and the investment of the owners in the business. The items of value owned or controlled by the business are called assets. Liabilities represent the claims of creditors against these assets. The value of the assets in excess of the total of the liabilities is called owners' equity, shareholders' equity, or stockholders' equity. In others words, owners' equity represents the owners' claim to the assets of a business net of its liabilities.

At any given time, the assets of a business equal the total claims against these assets by its creditors and owners. This relationship can be expressed by the balance sheet or accounting equation:

$$Assets = Liabilities + Owners' \ Equity$$

The balance sheet is usually prepared at regular intervals, such as the end of each month. The regular preparation of this summary help business owners to identify and analyze trends in the financial condition of the business.

What are the limitations of a balance sheet?

In examining a balance sheet, you should always be

aware of the information it fails to disclose and deficiencies in the information that it does disclose. For example, accountants do not include as assets certain items that are critical to the growth and well-being of the company, such as the value of its employees. Similarly, the value of trademarks or brand names is often omitted or shown as nominal amounts on the balance sheet.

The balance sheet seldom discloses the current market value of assets. Property, plant, and equipment is reflected at its original cost on the balance sheet; these figures may be obsolete and render the valuation shown on the balance sheet totally unrealistic.

Estimates and judgments often are necessary but may be highly inaccurate. For example, estimates are made to determine depreciation, collectibility of receivables, salability of inventory, pension obligations, warranty costs, and other items. Users frequently rely on accounting numbers reported in the balance sheet without realizing how important estimates are in producing these numbers.

What is the significance of stock dividends and stock splits?

A stock split is the issuance to stockholders of new shares of stock. For example, a two-for-one split gives each stockholder two new shares for each old share held. A stock dividend is simply a small stock split. For example, if a corporation issues a 5 percent stock dividend, the owner of 100 shares receives an additional five shares of stock. Essentially, all that happens with these operations is that the total number of shares outstanding increases, the price per share decreases proportionately, and the total value of the owners' common stock remains unchanged.

If nothing is gained through stock dividends or stock splits, what is a corporation's underlying motivation for such actions? For one thing, an unsupported tradition on Wall Street is that a stock price of between $25 and $50 is most appealing to investors; stock dividends or splits are ways of manipulating market price. In addition, stockholders seem to react positively to distributions of additional shares even if the total value of their holdings remains unchanged. The price of the stock seems "cheaper" after the split, especially in a company with rising earnings. Stock splits often occur following run-ups in the price of the stock; on the other hand, corporations often issue stock dividends when cash dividends are unaffordable.

What is the purpose of the statement of cash flows?

As of 1988, the statement of cash flows became a required statement, along with the income statement and balance sheet. This ruling was spurred by the dissatisfaction of many investors with reported earnings as a measure of a company's performance, because the final earnings figure is affected by the accounting methods used and may not be indicative of the underlying cash flows.

The primary purpose of the statement of cash flows is to report information about a company's cash receipts and cash payments during an accounting period. It is useful because it provides information about (1) sources of cash during the period; (2) uses of cash during the period; and (3) changes in cash balance during the period. Although this statement provides information about the current period's cash receipts and cash payments, it cannot be used alone to provide insight into future cash flows, because current cash receipts result from cash payments made in prior periods, while cash payments made currently frequently have the aim of increasing future cash receipts. As a result, the statement of cash flows must be used with the other financial statements to predict future cash flows.

What is the purpose of the income statement?

The income statement reports revenues and expenses incurred over a specific time period. After all expenses are subtracted from all revenues, the remainder is net income, or the "bottom line." (The terms income, earnings, and profits are used interchangeably by accountants.) The profit (or loss) is shown at the bottom of the income statement, as both a lump-sum figure and a per-share amount.

The income statement is important because it provides investors, creditors, and others with information to help predict the amount, timing, and uncertainty of future cash flows. (Investors should remember that, in the long run, there is a strong correlation between earnings growth and the performance of a company's common stock.) Accurate prediction of future cash flows permits the assessment of the economic value of the firm, the probability of loan repayment, and the likelihood of dividend payout.

What is the significance of earnings per share?

Earnings per share (EPS) is probably the most publicized and relied-upon financial statistic. In its simplest form, it is computed by dividing net income or earnings by the total number of common shares outstanding. The financial dailies report earnings for most listed and over-the-counter companies as they are announced. Corporations are required by the SEC to report EPS to their stockholders every three months; and these reported earnings can have at least a short-term impact on the price of a common stock, particularly when they differ from expectations.

EPS has been called a summary indicator because as a single item it communicates substantial information. However, misleading inferences can be drawn if the calculations that derive EPS on the income statement are ignored. Analysis of a company's total operations and financial condition requires more information that can be garnered by simply examining EPS.

What is leverage?

Financial leverage is the use of debt to magnify returns. Speculators in common stock attempt to multiply returns by supplementing their own funds with borrowed funds, and business firms use leverage to increase their income. Like individuals, they use debt to increase the resources available to generate future profits. Leveraging is successful as long as the money borrowed produces returns greater than the interest charges on the additional debt incurred. However, debt involves risk because the business commits itself to making fixed interest payments; if it cannot meet them, it will probably become insolvent.

How is the P/E ratio helpful to investors?

Is a stock cheap? Is the market as a whole undervalued? One of the most widely used tools to make this assessment is the price-earnings (P/E) ratio. A P/E ratio simply is a stock's price divided by the company's earnings per share over the most recent four quarters. A high P/E ratio indicates that the market expects exceptional earnings growth, and a low P/E ratio suggests that the market anticipates low earnings growth. The P/E ratio for each stock is listed in the daily stock tables of most major newspapers. Generally, the higher the P/E ratio, the more bullish investors are about a firm's prospects.

What is cash flow?

The definition of cash flow has never been totally clear either to accountants or to investors. In 1988, the accounting profession attempted to reduce the uncertainty by setting standards for and requiring a statement of cash flows. While not totally successful in resolving the debate over the definition, the ruling does provide stockholders and creditors with information they need to compute cash flow.

Cash flow is computed in several different ways. For example, cash flow can be defined by starting with net income and adding or subtracting certain noncash adjustments (as per the statement of cash flows). Many investors begin with this definition of cash flow but then deduct those capital expenditures needed to maintain the company's business. This definition is often called "free cash flow." Takeover specialists broaden the definition of cash flow by starting with pretax income, adding back interest expense, and deducting necessary capital expenditures. This definition gives a clearer picture of how much cash would be available to meet the debt in a takeover.

Are personal financial statements useful only to wealthy individuals?

The answer to this question is a definite no. Regardless of your income and wealth, personal financial statements are a necessary tool for effective financial planning. The balance sheet summarizes your financial condition at a certain point in time by reporting what you own, what you owe, and your financial net worth (what you own minus what you owe). The income statement provides a summary of the income you received and the money you spent over a given period of time, usually one year, thus evaluating your financial performance over time. Both of these financial statements are necessary to measure your financial position and monitor your progress in meeting your financial goals.

GLOSSARY

Accelerated Cost Recovery System (ACRS) A system used to depreciate the cost of long-term assets; used for tax purposes only.

Accelerated depreciation Methods of depreciation that recognize greater depreciation early in the life of the asset and less in the later years.

Acid-test (or Quick) ratio The sum of cash, marketable securities, and receivables divided by current liabilities.

Account A record summarizing the effects of transactions on asset, liability, and stockholders' equity components of a company.

Accounts payable Amounts owed for the purchase of goods and services.

Accounts receivable Amounts due from sales on credit.

Accounts receivable turnover ratio A financial ratio computed by dividing net credit sales by average accounts receivable.

Accounting equation An algebraic expression of financial postion: Assets = Liabilities + Owners' or Stockholders' Equity.

Accrued liabilities Liabilities incurred but not yet recorded.

Accumulated depreciation The total past depreciation on a specific asset.

Additional paid-in capital The amount invested by the owners over and above the par value of capital stock.

Allowance for doubtful accounts The estimated total of the yet unidentified accounts receivable that will not be collected.

Amortization The systematic allocation of the cost of an intangible asset to expense over its useful life.

Assets The items of value that the business owns or controls.

Auditor's opinion A report by an independent CPA as to the fairness of presentation of the financial statements.

Balance sheet A financial statement that discloses the financial position of a firm at a particular point in time.

Balance Sheet Ratios Ratios of numbers reported on the balance sheet.

Book of Original Entry A journal in which each transaction is originally recorded.

Book Value For an asset, cost less accumulated depreciation or amortization; for each share of common stock, common stockholders' equity divided by the outstanding shares.

Bookkeeping The recording of transactions.

Capital Stock The amount invested by the owners of the business; a general term for common stock.

Cash Cash and cash equivalents.

Cash dividends Distributions to stockholders of cash.

Cash Flow Statement A financial statement disclosing the cash receipts and cash payments during an accounting period.

Common Stock The stock representing the basic ownership interest in a corporation.

Conservatism A principle of accounting that requires accountants to choose that alternative least likely to overstate assets or income.

Consistency An accounting principle that requires accounting procedures to be applied consistently from period to period.

Consolidated Financial Statements Combined financial statements of a parent and its subsidiaries.

Contra-asset Account An account reducing asset balances in the balance sheet.

Contingent Liabilities A potential liability whose outcome depends upon some future event.

Corporate Bonds A written agreement whereby the corporation borrows money and promises to repay a specific sum on a future date and to make periodic interest payments.

Corporation A form of business organization recognized as a separate entity distinct from its owners.

Cost of Goods Sold The cost of the inventory or goods that have sold to customers. This is an expense on the income statement.

Credit An entry on the right side of a ledger account.

Current Assets The more liquid assets of the business.

Current Liabilities Debts payable within one year.

Current Maturities of Long-term Debt The debt due within one year.

Current Ratio The ratio of current assets divided by current liabilities.

Debentures An unsecured bond.

Debit An entry on the left side of a ledger account.

Debt/Equity Ratio Total liabilities divided by total owners' or stockholders' equity.

Debt Ratio Total liabilities divided by the sum of liabilities and owners' or stockholders' equity.

Deferred Income Taxes An account used to record the difference between taxes expense per the books and tax payable per the tax return.

Defined Benefit Plan A pension plan in which the benefits are specified under the pension plan.

Defined Contribution Plan A pension plan in which the contributions are specified under the pension plan.

Depletion The allocation of the cost of natural resources to expense as they are used.

Depreciation The decline in utility of an asset as a result of the passage of time.

Discontinued Operations A segment of a business that is sold, abandoned, or disposed.

Dividend A distribution of the earnings of a corporation to its shareholders.

Dividend Yield Percentage The annual cash dividend

per share divided by the current market price of the stock.

Double-declining-balance Depreciation An accelerated method of depreciation in which the straight-line rate is doubled.

Earnings Per Share Net income or earnings per share of common stock.

Employer's Pension Obligation The pension benefits payable to employees after they retire.

Expense Dollar amount of the costs incurred in producing revenues.

Extraordinary Items Gains or losses that are unusual in nature and infrequent in occurrence.

Financial Accounting An area of accounting that is primarily concerned with external reporting.

Financial Accounting Standards Board (FASB) A private-sector body that issues accounting standards.

Financial Leverage The use of debt financing to increase profits.

Financial Statements The financial reports reporting the financial position and results of operations.

Financing Activities Funds received from the company's owners or creditors.

First-in, First-out (FIFO) An inventory costing method in which costs are assigned to goods in the order that the goods are received.

First Mortgage Bonds Bonds secured by specific assets.

Fixed Expenses Expenses whose total remains unchanged regardless of changes in output.

Full Disclosure An accounting principle that requires accountants to strive to disclose information relevant to the decision needs of users.

Fully Diluted Earnings Per Share Computation of earnings per share reflecting the effects of the hypothetical exercise of all dilutive financial securities.

Fundamental Analysis A method of security valuation that attempts to measure the intrinsic value of a security and relies heavily on financial statements and economic trends.

Funded Pension Plan A plan in which a company sets aside funds for future pension benefits by making payments to a funding agency.

Generally Accepted Accounting Principles (GAAP) The conventions, rules, and procedures underlying accounting for financial reporting purposes.

Going Concern The assumption that a company will have an indefinite life.

Goodwill The amount paid in excess of the current value of the assets less liabilities acquired.

Gross Margin The difference between sales and cost of goods sold.

Gross Profit The difference between sales and cost of goods sold. Same as gross margin.

Gross Profit Margin Gross profit or margin divided by sales.

Historical Cost The original cost of an asset.

Income Bonds Bonds on which interest is payable only if the corporation operates at a profit.

Income statement A financial statement that discloses the amount of income earned during an accounting period.

Income Tax Payable The amount due to the Internal Revenue Service.

Intangible Assets Long-term assets that lack physical substance.

Interest Expense The cost of using borrowed funds.

Interperiod Tax Allocations Allocation of income taxes among different accounting periods.

Intrinsic Value of a Security The price at which a security should sell under normal market conditions.

Inventory Goods acquired for resale.

Inventory Turnover Ratio The cost of goods sold divided by average inventory.

Investing Activities The making and collecting of loans and acquiring and disposing of plant and equipment.

Investments Securities held for the long-term.

Journal A chronological record of each transaction.

Last-in, First-out (LIFO) An inventory valuation method in which the costs are assigned to inventory in the reverse order in which the goods are received.

Ledger A book or file of all of a company's accounts.

Liabilities The claims against the assets of the business.

Liquidity The closeness of an asset to cash.

Long-term Liabilities Liabilities paid after one year.

Management Ratios Ratios that evaluate the efficiency and effectiveness of management.

Marketable Debt Securities Highly liquid equity securities.

Marketable Equity Securities Highly liquid equity securities.

Matching Principle An accounting principle that requires revenues to be recognized when earned and the expenses incurred in producing those revenues to be recognized in the same period.

Materiality The relative significance of an item to an informed user.

Monetary Assets Cash and claims to cash.

Money Measurement The principle that business transactions should be measured in terms of money.

Net Income The difference between the sum of revenues and gains and the sum of expenses and losses.

Net Income from Operations (Operating Income) Net income less cost of goods sold an operating expenses.

Net Profit Margin Net profit or income divided by net sales.

Net Sales Sales less returns, allowances, and discounts.

Notes Payable Debts evidenced by a promissory note.

Operating activities Cash effects of transactions that enter into the determination of net income.

Operating Profit Margin Net income from operations divided by net sales.

Owners' Equity The amount supplied to the business by its owners.

Par Value An arbitrary fixed amount per share printed on the stock certificate.

Parent Company A company that owns most of the common stock of another company.

Partnership A legal entity formed by two or more owners.

Payout Ratio Cash dividends divided by net income.

Pension Plan A contract between the company and its employees whereby the company agrees to make payments after the employee retires.

Percentage-of-completion Revenue Recognition A method for recognizing revenue and profit according to the extent of completion.

Permanent Difference The difference between income tax expense and income tax payable does not reverse in future periods.

Personal Balance Sheet The assets, liabilities, and owners' equity of an individual.

Personal Financial Statements Financial reports prepared for an individual.

Personal Income Statement A report listing revenues and expenditures.

Preferred Stock Stock having certain rights over common stock.

Prepaid Expenses Expenses paid in advance.

Pretax Accounting Income Net income before income taxes have been deducted.

Primary Earnings Per Share Earnings per share reflecting the hypothetical exercise of all common stock equivalents.

Prior Period Adjustments Corrections of errors made in prior period financial statements.

Probable A contingency that is likely to occur.

Property, Plant, and Equipment Long-term, tangible assets whose life extends beyond one year.

Proprietorship A business with a single owner.

Qualified Opinion A report issued by CPAs that takes exception to the fairness of the presentation of the financial statements.

Quarterly Financial Statements Financial statements issued every three months.

Ratio Analysis A method of expressing financial statement relationships.

Ratio of Return on Assets Net income divided by total assets.

Reasonably Possible A contingency which is less than likely to occur but more than a remote possibility.

Remote A contingency unlikely to occur.

Retained Earnings The earnings of the corporation that have been retained for use in the business rather than distributed to the shareholders as dividends.

Return on Equity (ROE) Net income divided by owners' or stockholders' equity.

Securities and Exchange Commission (SEC) A federal agency that has the power to prescribe accounting practices for companies that issue publicly traded securities.

Selling, General, and Administrative Expenses The operating expenses of the firm.

Shareholders or Stockholders Equity The summation of a corporation's contributed capital and retained earnings.

Statement of Earnings (Profit and Loss Statement) The same as the income statement.

Statement of Retained Earnings A financial statement that discloses the changes in the retained earnings account during the accounting period.

Statements of Financial Accounts Standards (SFAS) Accounting rules issued by the Financial Accounting Standards Board.

Stock Dividend A distribution to stockholders in the form of additional shares of common stock.

Stock split An increase in the number of outstanding shares accompanied by a proportionate decrease in the par or stated value.

Straight-Line Depreciation A method of depreciation that recognized the same amount of depreciation expense each period.

Subsidiary A corporation wholly or partly owned by another company.

Sum-of-the-year's-digits Depreciation An accelerated

method of depreciation in which a smaller fraction is applied to cost less salvage each period.

"T" Account An account that has a T-shaped form.

Tangible Assets Assets that have a physical substance.

Taxable Income The income reportable to the Internal Revenue Service.

Transaction Business events recorded in the financial records.

Technical Analysis A method of predicting future stock prices by analyzing past prices.

Temporary Difference Differences between income tax expense and income tax payable that will reverse at some future date.

Temporary Investment The same as a marketable security.

Treasury Stock The repurchase by a company of its own outstanding stock.

Units of Production Depreciation A depreciation method in which depreciation expense varies with usage of the asset.

Unqualified Opinion A report issued by CPAs stating that the financial statements are a fair presentation of the company's financial position and earnings for the year.

Variable Expenses Expenses whose amount varies directly with changes in output.

Working Capital The excess of total current assets over current liabilities.

INDEX